OPTION TRADING

STOCK MARKET

INVESTING

BUNDLE

Crash Course for Beginners:
How to Create Passive Income to Get Fresh Money to Buy and Sell Options

Anthony Sinclair

Table of Contents

BOOK1: STOCK MARKET INVESTING

INTRODUCTION..9

BEGINNERS..17

CHAPTER 1. THE BASICS OF INVESTING IN STOCKS........................18
    How Does the Stock Market Work?..22
    Basic Terms and Concepts...25

CHAPTER 2. STEPS TO EVALUATE YOUR FINANCIAL HEALTH, SETTING, GOALS (WHAT TO CONSIDER BEFORE OPENING A NEW ACCOUNT)   32
    Where..34
    Seek Liquidity...35
    Dealing with Debts..35
    Having an Emergency Fund..39
    Consider Additional Sources of Income.......................................40
    Net Worth and Changes Over Time..41
    Are You Ready to Invest?...42
    Determining Your Financial Goals..42

CHAPTER 3. RISKS IN INVESTING IN STOCKS...................................44
    Emotional and Person Risk..46
    Risk of Loss of Capital...50
    Market and Economic Risk...51

- Interest Rate Risk..51
- Political Risk and Government...53
- Inflation Risk...54
- Taxes and Commissions..54
- Risk vs. Return..55
- Managing Risk..56

CHAPTER 4. HOW TO INVEST IN STOCKS (HOW TO BUY YOUR FIRST STOCK)..58
- How to Get Start..60
- Planning and Meeting Goals...61
- Choosing an Investment Method..63
- Choosing a Stockbroker..65
- Opening an Account...66
- Buying and Selling Stocks...68

CHAPTER 5. WHEN TO BUY AND SELL STOCK...............................70
- When to Sell a Stock...72
- When to Buy a Stock...77
- Stock Order Types...80

CHAPTER 6. HOW TO GENERATE PASSIVE INCOME FROM THE STOCK MARKET..84
- Yield...86
- Dividend...87
- Dividend Growth..87
- DRIPS and Reinvesting...88
- Exchange-Traded Funds..89
- Alternative Investments..89
- When to Cash Out..91
- Fundamentals Always Matter...92
- Bond Investing...92

CHAPTER 7. THE MAIN MISTAKES OF A BEGINNER........................94
- Failure to Understand the Trade...96

Impatience..97
Failure to Diversify..98
Getting Too Connected with a Certain Company........................99
Investment Turnover..99
Timing the Market..100
Trading with Emotions..100
Setting Unrealistic Expectations..................................101
Using Borrowed Money..101

CRASH COURSE..103

CHAPTER 8. INSIDER TRICKS USED BY PROFESSIONAL TRADERS..104
Insider Trading..106
Quantity also Matters..109
Congressional Insiders..109
Stock Buybacks..109
Stock Splits..111

CHAPTER 9. TIPS AND TRICKS FOR SUCCESSFUL STOCKS TRADING..114
Always Be Informed..116
Buy Low, Sell High..116
Scalping..117
Short Selling..118
Identify the Pattern..118
Look at the Results..119
Look at the Company Name..120
Understand the Company Better..................................120
Don't Trust Mails..122
Understand the Corrections..122
Hire a Broker Only If Necessary..................................123

Diversify Your Risks.. 124
Money Movement.. 124
Look at the Stock Volume.. 125

CHAPTER 10. ADVICE TO MINIMIZING LOSSES AND MAXIMIZING GAINS.. 126

What Other Factors Affect the Trading Process?....................... 130
Options Trading — Losing Before Winning................................ 130

CHAPTER 11. TAX IMPLICATION AND HOW TO REDUCE THEIR IMPACT ON YOUR EARNINGS... 136

Capital Gains... 138
Dividend Income... 139
Individual Retirement Accounts.. 140
Expenses.. 141
Understanding Your Brokerage Account and Statement........... 141
What is a Brokerage Account?... 142
Type of Investments a Brokerage Account Can Hold................. 143
Cash Brokerage Accounts and Margin Brokerage Accounts...... 145
Limits of Money You Can Deposit in a Brokerage Account....... 146
How Many Brokerage Accounts Can One Have?....................... 146
Difference between a Discount Broker and a Full-Service Broker... 146
Understanding Your Broker's Statement..................................... 148

CHAPTER 12. WHAT TO DO AND WHAT TO BUY IN A DOWN MARKET... 152

Buy Depressed Assets... 154
Dollar-Cost Averaging... 156
Buy Self Liquidating Assets.. 159
Smart Money Valuation.. 159

CHAPTER 13. HOW TO USE BOTH MACROECONOMIC AND MICROECONOMIC ANALYSIS... 162

Macro-Economic Analysis.. 164
Interest Rates.. 165

The Cyclical Nature of an Industry 166
Stock Market Index 166
Industry-Wide Research 167
Micro- Economic Analysis 167

CHAPTER 14.   HOW TO CREATE A SECURE FINANCIAL FUTURE 170

How to Choose the Right Stocks to Invest In 175
Setting an Investment Objective 176
Factors to Consider in Choosing a Stock 177

CHAPTER 15.   STOCK MARKET STRATEGIES FOR PROFITABLE INVESTING 188

The Business Know 190
Evite Fraud 191
A Stock Broker Notice 191
Train Yourself 192
Take Stock Exchange Tools 193
Continue to Train 193

CHAPTER 16.   COVID-19 EFFECTS ON WORKING WITH STOCKS 196

CONCLUSION 206

Table of Contents

BOOK2: OPTIONS TRADING

INTRODUCTION 7

BEGINNERS 13

CHAPTER 1. WHAT ARE OPTIONS TRADING AND THE BEST MARKET 14

- Call Options 17
- Put Options 19
- Long As Opposed to Short Options 20

CHAPTER 2. HOW MUCH CAPITAL DO YOU NEED TO TRADE 22

- How to Start Options Trading 25

CHAPTER 3. BASIC OPTIONS STRATEGIES 32

- Collars 34
- Credit Spreads 34
- Covered Calls 35
- Cash Naked Put 35
- Long Call 35
- Short Call Option 36
- Long Put Option 36
- Iron Condor 37
- Married Put 37
- Cash Covered Put 38
- Long Butterfly 38
- Short Butterfly 38
- Long Straddle 39
- Short Straddle 39
- Reverse Iron Condor 40
- Iron Butterfly Spread 40

Short Bull Ratio..40
Strap Straddle..40
Strap Strangle..41
Limit Your Risk...41

CHAPTER 4. RISKS MANAGEMENT IN OPTIONS 46

Stock Risk – Dividends and Buy-in Risk..50
Pin Risk..51
Forward Risk..52
Irrelevance of the Greeks..52
Expiring at a Short Strike..54

CHAPTER 5. VOLATILITY IN THE MARKET 56

Historical Volatility..58
Implied Volatility...58
The Impact of Volatility on Options Trades...60
How to Compute Historical Volatility..61
How to Compute Implied Volatility...63

CHAPTER 6. TYPICAL BEGINNERS MISTAKES IN OPTIONS 66

Ignoring the Statistics Behind Options Trading....................................68
Not Being Adaptable..70
Ignoring the Probability..72
Not Considering Exotic Options...73
Not Keeping Earnings and Dividend Dates in Mind..............................75

CHAPTER 7. IMPORTANT TRADING PRINCIPLES TO FOLLOW 78

Ensure Good Money Management...80
Ensure That Risks and Rewards Are Balanced.....................................83
Develop a Consistent Monthly Options Trading System........................84
Consider a Brokerage Firm That is Right for Your Level of Options Expertise..84
Broker Services and Features..86
Commissions and Other Fees..87
Ensure That Exits are automated...88

CRASH COURSE   91

CHAPTER 8.   BUY AN EQUITY AT A LOWER PRICE   92

Trading Beams with Large Margins..94
Purchase Zones..95
The Stop..96
Profit Taking..98
Anticipation..99
The Time-Break-Out Rule..101
Price Gaps..101

CHAPTER 9.   OPTIONS PRICING   104

Strike Price and Underlying Price..107
Factors That Affect an Option's Price..109
History of the Black-Scholes Model..110
Stock Price..111
Strike Price..112
Type of Option...113
Time to expiration..114
Interest Rates..114
Dividends..116
Volatility..116

CHAPTER 10.   TIPS AND TRICKS IN STOCKS   118

The Price of Any Stock Can Move in 3 Basic Directions....................120
Before Buying a Call or Put Option, Look at the Underlying Stock's Chart..122
Chart Readings and Buying Call Options...123
Chart Readings and Buying Put Options..123
Chart Readings for Purchase of Call and Put Options.....................124
Find Out the Breakeven Point Before Buying Your Options.............124
Calculating the Breakeven Point...125
If You Are Dealing with Call and Put Options, Embrace the Underlying Stock's Trend..126
When Trading Options, Watch Out for Earnings Release Dates.....127

CHAPTER 11.   HOW TO DOUBLE OR TRIPLE YOUR RETURNS   123

   Buy Low and Sell High 130
   Focus on Not Losing Money Rather Than on Making Money 131
   Develop a Sense of Sentiment Analysis 132
   Learn from Your Competitors 136
   Cash-Out 137
   Take a Break and Have Fun 138

CHAPTER 12.   HOW TO BECOME A MILLIONAIRE
WITH OPTION TRADING   140

   Writing Options 142
   The Straddle Strategy 143
   The Collar Strategy 144
   The Strangle Strategy 144
   Options Trading is Quite Profitable 146
   The Most Profitable Options Trading Strategy 147
   Consistently Profitable Strategies – Selling Puts & Credit Spreads 148
   Overall Best Options Trading Strategy 149
   A Closer Look at Naked Puts 151
   ROI or Return on Investment 152

CHAPTER 13.   HOW COVID-19 WILL AFFECT
OPTION TRADING   154

   Equity Trading is Also on the Rise 160

CONCLUSION   164

STOCK MARKET INVESTING

A Crash Course Guide to Trading from Beginners to Expert:

How to Create Passive Income to Get Fresh Money to Buy and Sell Options

Anthony Sinclair

Introduction

The fact is that for most young people, investing might not be the most important thing in their lives. Until they get older and established in a career, saving and investing for retirement may not be at the top of their priority list; there are other things that might seem more pressing and exciting at this stage in life.

When you're young, you have limited resources to invest. You're also still trying to figure out who you are — what kind of career or education you want to pursue, and how much risk you want to take with your money. For these reasons, it's not a good idea to jump into the stock market before you have a better handle on your financial circumstances and goals.

This doesn't mean you'll never be able to invest in the stock market, but it does mean that you're a long way off from making a decision that will have a major impact on your life. Until then, there are plenty of other ways to get started with investing and he stock market without getting ahead of yourself.

It is difficult to believe there was a time when the stock market didn't exist. The stock market is on the tip of nearly everyone's tongue. Even individuals who do not invest at least know it exists. It is largely understood that the New York Stock Exchange is the biggest market of them all, with any company listed on it that wants to be recognized globally. However, how did the stock market come to fruition? Is there more than the NYSE (New York Stock Exchange)? There are more exchanges and it started with the Real Merchants of Venice and British Coffeehouses.

Europe was filled with moneylenders that filled in the gaps of the larger banks. Moneylenders would trade between themselves. One lender might get rid of a high-risk, high-interest loan by trading it to another lender. Moneylenders also purchased government debt. In a natural evolution, lenders started selling debts to customers who were looking to invest.

Investors also put their money into ships and crews. Most of the time-limited liability companies would go on a single voyage to gain merchandise from Asia and the East Indies as a way to bring a profit to the investor. New companies were usually formed for the next voyage to reduce the risk of investing in ships that could end up in disaster. The East India companies worked with investors by providing dividends made from the goods that came in. Stocks were now in place, where the first joint-stock company was created. At the time, there were royal charters that made competition impossible and thus, investors gained huge profits.

It was not without its troubles. The stock market is based on economic stability. When instability reigns the stock market can crash because there is no liquidity, which is what happened during the Great Depression. Everyone saw the banks failing due to debts and little liquidity, which in turn caused others to suffer, businesses too close, and stock shares to plummet.

The stock market formed from a need to have a place to conduct the business of selling shares, which was already happening. Governments needed to regulate stock sales, and prevent issues like the SSC crash. Nevertheless, there was also greed on behalf of wealthy citizens. There was a clear way to earn money from someone else's labor, thus the stock exchanges were started.

Investors and traders sell stocks after the IPO based on the perceived value. A company's value can go up or down, which is where investors make their money. A company's stock price that rises can provide a profit. If an investor has purchased those shares and the price or company value decreases, then the investor will lose money. In addition, the investors and traders will push the price in an up or down direction.

Investors have one of two goals: investing in the short or the long term. A long-term investment is based on a stock continuing to rise in price. A short-term investment is to gain quick cash and pulling out before the stock price decreases.

Mature companies offer dividends to their shareholders. If you have stocks, then you are a shareholder in a company. If you hold the stocks long enough and have enough stock in a company, you can vote on new board members. Dividends are company profits that you get a cut of.

Investors will make money on the price fluctuations and the dividends. A seller is often trying to gain a profit by selling to a new buyer. The new buyer is also trying to buy as low as possible so that when the stock price continues to increase, they will make a profit.

The profit is calculated by taking the initial buy price and subtracting it from the closing or sale price. For example, if you buy into Google at $400 and wait for it to go up to $600, then the profit is $200 per share.

Sellers can push the price down due to supply and demand. This financial market works based on supply and demand.

You should already know that in economics when there is an oversupply of a product, the price is low. There is no demand for the product; therefore, a company or in this case a stock is not of interest.

When there is an undersupply of something like a stock, the demand is high. With more interested parties, the price will continue to increase.

If there is an even amount of supply and demand, then equality exists and there is no movement to see.

For the stock market, when too many people sell a stock, the price will decline. When too many people buy a stock, the price will continue to rise. If there is an equal number of shares and interest, then the price usually trades sideways because there is a balance.

As you learn about the stock market, you will hear the word volume, often. Volume is the number of shares that change hands on a daily basis. Millions of shares can be traded on the stock exchange in a day as investors attempt to make money from increasing or decreasing prices.

The stock market works based on the interest or volume of traders. If a stock does not have any volume or very little, then it is not being actively traded, thus the price is not moving. Traders such as market makers get into the market in order to buy or sell stocks for companies with low volume. They do not stop a stock from rising or falling. Instead, market makers just trying to garner interest in the company's stock.

When it comes to the stock market and traders, most individuals are looking for high-volume traders, with fluctuating prices. They get in, make a profit, and get out finding the next big profit.

BEGINNERS

Chapter 1. The Basics of Investing in Stocks

Delayed gratification is a strong suit that few have and this is why investing has always been a challenge for many. You want to make money but not in a decade or a couple of years, but right now. Ponzi schemes aside, profitable investments that can actually build you wealth for a lifetime take time and lots of patience. These two things are probably the most important tools that any beginner in stock market investing needs to be aware of.

Our motivations for investing may differ but ultimately all investments have one goal in common; to make a return or profit on the investment. You may be eyeing early retirement, you may be in it for financial freedom or maybe you are just sick of having your money sitting in a savings account attracting point nothing interest. Regardless of what your goals are, the idea behind investing is that you use your money to make more money.

The stock market presents a unique opportunity for both retail and corporate investors because anyone can do it at any scale. You can invest as little as $1000 or as much as a million dollars. There are room and opportunity for everyone to get in and make a decent return on their investment. That said, the stock market is not the way to go if you want quick money. Stocks like most other investments have one thing in common; they depend on the power of time.

Time is your biggest ally when it comes to investing. If you have been waiting for a magical moment when you will have "enough" money to start investing, the bad news is that you will probably never have "enough" money and the other bad news is that the right time to start investing was yesterday.

A common misconception that most people have is that you need to have a lot of money to start investing. In actual fact, people who invest do not necessarily have more money than you, they simply make investing a priority. And because they make investing a priority, they end up having more money than you. See how that works?

Unlike consumption, investment takes money out of your pocket and puts it towards your future. When you can think of investment as an insurance policy to safeguard your financial future then the decision on when and if to invest becomes pretty much a no-brainer. Nobody wants to be cash-strapped forever or have to work themselves to the grave because they did not put their money to work when they had the chance.

The beauty of this golden age of technology that we live in is that anyone with the will and determination to do so can access all the tools they need to start investing in the stock market. This ease of accessibility coupled with its affordability has made the stock market increasingly popular with retail investors. With just a few a hundred dollars you can find an online brokerage at the click of a button and get started as an investor in the stock market. Yes, it is that easy. Before you jump on the bandwagon, however, it is important to understand what you are investing in. The natural starting point is, of course, understanding how the stock market works.

How Does the Stock Market Work?

It is no coincidence that most people who have wealth have a big part of this wealth invested in stocks. Stocks carry their fair share of risks for any investor but when done right, stock market investing can be one of the most efficient ways to build and retain wealth.

A stock market is an exchange where people trade by buying and selling shares on traded companies. Once you have bought shares in a company your stock gives you ownership of a small part of that company. With this ownership, the value of your investment will be determined by the movements of the price of the company's shares. If for instance, you bought Apple stocks and the price moves up while you are holding the stock then the value of your investment increases. On the other hand, if the price of the Apple stocks decreases while you are holding the stocks, the value of your investment decreases.

The price of a stock is driven by the forces of supply and demand. Naturally, when the demand for a particular stock is higher than the supply, the price of that stock will increase. In much the same way, when the supply is higher than the demand, then the price of that stock will decrease. In essence, the stock price is a reflection of the value as set by the market conditions. When you buy a stock as an investor, your general goal is to make money when the price of the stock increases. This is why a big part of investing in the stock market is knowing how to select the right stocks to buy.

When the price of the shares you have appreciates, you can sell your shares at a profit. This means that you will get a return on your investment and you can reinvest your capital back into the market or you can cash out. The beauty of stock market investing is that there is usually no limit to how long you can hold your investment. You can keep your shares for 20 years or you can choose to sell them when the share price appreciates. This will ultimately depend on what your end goal is.

Price appreciation is not the only way to make money in the stock market. Dividends are payments made out to shareholders when a company makes a profit. This means that depending on the type of shares you have, you will receive dividends from the company whose shares you hold.

For instance, if you bought Tesla stocks and the company pays out dividends quarterly to their shareholders, you will get a percentage of these dividends based on the value of your shares. You can choose to take these dividends as a cash payment or you can choose to reinvest them back into the company by buying more shares.

It is important to note that not all companies pay dividends. This means that if you want to make money in the stock market by earning regular dividends, you will need to understand the type of stocks to buy and which company's stocks will get you dividends.

Stock exchanges like the NYSE (New York Stock Exchange), NASDAQ, the Tokyo Stock Exchange are some of the largest exchanges. However, stocks are also sold in over-the-counter markets where they trade directly through brokers and not in open exchanges like the NYSE. These markets are referred to as secondary markets where investors trade stocks by buying and selling amongst themselves.

Basic Terms and Concepts

- **Stocks**

    A stock is a share of ownership in a company. Stocks are also referred to as shares. When you buy a stock you acquire a fraction of ownership of the company whose shares you have bought. When you buy stocks, you become a shareholder in a particular company and the percentage or size of your shares will determine the dividends you can earn.

Investors in the stock market can make money from their stocks in different ways. You can earn money in the form of dividends paid out on the shares you own. You can also earn money by selling your shares or stocks.

- **Common Stock**

Common stocks give you ownership of a company based on the number of shares you own. Common stocks are the most basic type of shares to own and they entitle you to dividends where applicable and voting rates proportionate to the shares you own.

- **Preferred Stock**

Preferred stocks entitle you to a fixed dividend rate for your shares. With this type of stock, you earn dividends before shareholders who have common stock but you do not get voting rights. Unlike shareholders of common stocks, preferred stocks give you a guarantee that you will receive dividends on your stock.

- **Penny Stocks**

A penny stock is a stock that trades for less than $5 per share. Penny stocks are typically short-term holdings where you want to take advantage of price movements in volatile markets. Penny stocks investing works for short-term investors who do not plan to hold the stocks for long periods.

- **Blue Chip Stocks**

Blue-chip stocks are shares of large established corporations that have solid reputations in the market. Blue-chip stocks are characterized by solid balance sheets and steady cash flows. Most blue-chip stocks have a history of earning increasing dividends for their shareholders. These types of stocks are ideal for long-term investors who want to hold stocks for long periods.

- **Primary Market**

In a primary market, companies sell their shares directly to investors. In most cases, companies in primary markets sell to corporations and institutions rather than to individual investors. Hedge funds, mutual funds, and similar investors are typically the kind of investors that buy shares directly from companies in primary markets.

- **Secondary Markets**

In a secondary market, investors buy and sell shares amongst themselves. Individual investors buy shares in secondary markets. In this type of market, you can choose to buy shares of a particular company or a mix of different companies' shares in exchange-traded funds or EFTs.

- **Over-the-Counter Markets**

OTC markets are where companies that are not listed in exchanges like NYSE trade their shares. In OTC markets there is no public price for the shares and the value of the transaction is dependent on the buyer and seller.

- **Bid**

A bid is a price at which you want to buy the share.

- **Ask**

The ask is the price at which the seller wants to sell the share at

- **Spread**

The spread is the difference between the bids and sell prices of a stock. If you want to buy a stock at $50 and the buyer wants to sell it at $45, the spread, in this case, is $5.

- **Volatility**

Volatility refers to the movement of share prices in the market. When the price fluctuates widely within short periods of time then it is said to be highly volatile. The higher the volatility of a particular share, the higher the risk associated with it and also the higher the profit potential.

- **Dividend**

A dividend is the percentage of a company's earnings that is paid out to shareholders. Dividends can be paid out annually or quarterly depending on the company. Not all companies pay dividends to the shareholders.

- **Broker**

A broker is a trader who buys and sells shares for an investor for a fee or commission.

- **Bear Market**

A bear market refers to a downward trend in the market where stock prices are falling

- **Bull Market**

A bull market refers to an upward trend in the market where stock prices are rising.

- **Beta**

Beta is the measurement of the price of a stock relative to the movement of the whole market. If a stock moves 1.5 points for every 1-point move in the market, then it has a beta of 1.5.

- **Index**

An index is a measure that is used as a benchmark to gauge market performance. Some of the most famous indices include the Dow Jones and the S&P 500.

Chapter 2. Steps to Evaluate Your Financial Health, Setting, Goals (What to Consider Before Opening a New Account)

There are many ways to go about investing and knowing which path to take can be a daunting process. You can narrow down the possibilities to a strategy that works for you by evaluating your current financial situation. This should be done before you enter into your first trade. To be successful, an investor needs a clear picture of where they are going. Keep in mind this is not a one-time event. You should reevaluate your financial situation on an annual basis since it's going to be changing. When you find yourself in a different financial situation, your investment strategies will change over time.

Where

Establishing a starting point is the first step. You don't have to be a financial wizard, but you need to be aware of your present situation before jumping in and buying stocks. Consider the following scenario. An investor with a large personal debt that has an interest rate of 17% keeps putting money in the stock market, hoping to build wealth over time. That sounds reasonable, but most market returns are, going to be in the range of 5-10%. That means that someone in this situation is actually losing money.

Seek Liquidity

We are going to recommend that you look for assets you can sell.

The money can be used to pay debts, back taxes, or to seed investment capital. You'll want to list all of your assets by liquidity, which means how easily they can be converted into cash. You'll also want to consider how much cash you can raise by selling each item if you were to sell it. A house might have a lot more value than a television set, but you might sell the television set in 24 hours while you'd have to wait months to sell the house.

Dealing with Debts

Taking care of debts is one of the first things that a budding investor needs to do. While you might be anxious to get started with a large-scale investment plan if you have debts to take care of you might want to put it off. So, the first step in preparing your investment plan is to create a simple balance sheet. You don't have to be an accountant, and you're only doing this for yourself, but it needs to be honest and accurate.

You're going to want to put together a listing of all of your assets and liabilities. When compiling assets, include everything of value that you could possibly sell. This could be a computer that you're not using, a dusty TV in a room nobody goes into very often, or an old guitar. Selling things, you don't need can help you pay off debts faster and raise investment capital. You might object that you wouldn't raise much money but imagine having an extra $500 to $1,000 to start off with.

When listing your liabilities, you're going to want to know how much debt you have, what the interest rates are, and what your monthly payments are.

Monthly payments are less important than interest rates. Once you've listed all of your debts, you'll want to develop a plan to pay them off in a reasonable amount of time. There are many calculators available online, and you can also read many books on how to pay off debt. The series of books by debt guru Dave Ramsey is highly recommended. Here is an example of a good debt calculator:

https://www.creditkarma.com/calculators/ debt_repayment/

You can use this calculator to figure out how long it will take to pay off a debt for a given monthly payment. You can enter the interest rate, and the time frame you would like along with the monthly payment you're willing to make. Start off with the current minimum payment in order to determine the time required to pay off the debt and work up from there.

In this example, we considered a $21,000 debt with a high 11% interest rate. Paying $450 a month would take five years to pay off the debt.

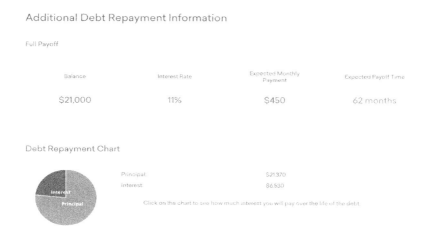

That isn't a good situation to be in — do you want to saddle yourself with a $21,000 debt for five years?

When you have listed all of your debts, then you can prioritize them. In order to make the most progress in the shortest amount of time, it can be helpful to tackle the smallest debts first. This not only helps you get rid of your debt faster, but it will also have psychological benefits as you improve your financial situation.

If you have back taxes, you should make these a priority. The reason is that the government tacks on lots of fees and penalties, and if the tax debt is allowed to sit around, it can grow substantially in size. Get payment plans arranged to take care of these debts before they become unmanageable.

Take a look at your spending habits. Having material goods now isn't important if you plan to become a successful investor. You will be able to buy that BMW or Mercedes you want later when you can really afford it. For now, your focus should be on being able to direct your financial resources into your investments so that you can grow your wealth over time. Expensive toys, like a new car, can be a large financial drain. If you have car loans, consider getting out of the car and into a used car that is reliable but costs a lot less. From this point forward, don't use debt to finance purchases. Keep a credit card on hand for emergencies, but don't use it to buy things like books or groceries that should be paid for using cash. If you can't pay for something with cash, it can wait.

Having an Emergency Fund

Life is never fair, and we are all going to encounter emergencies.

Recent studies have shown that most Americans don't have enough cash on hand to pay a $500 bill. If you are in that situation, you need to rectify it before you jump in with a large-scale investment plan. Remember that paying off debt first is always the priority. Debt is a sink that sucks important financial resources down the drain that could be used for other purposes. However, it's important to start putting money away for an emergency fund to be prepared for the unexpected — and being able to pay for it without having to take on more debt. Or worse, getting into a situation where you can't get credit but still need to find money to pay emergency bills. Set aside a small amount of money that you can start depositing into a savings account that you won't touch unless there is an emergency. Over time, the goal should be to have enough cash on hand to take care of emergency bills ranging up to $5,000 and to have funds on hand to cover times when you might be unemployed.

Consider Additional Sources of Income

If you have a large amount of debt or find yourself in a situation where coming up with a significant amount of money to invest is difficult, you should consider taking action to increase your income. There are many paths to consider. You can start by looking for a higher-paying job.

Alternatively, you can look into taking a second job, at least until you are in a better financial situation. Another approach that can be used is to either take on "gigs" or short-term contract work.

This can be done online or by doing some side work with companies like Uber. You can even look into starting your own online business to generate more income.

This doesn't have to be a permanent situation, but you are going to want to get to a place where you are debt-free and can put $1,000 or more into the stock market every month.

Net Worth and Changes Over Time

When you've gathered everything together, you'll want to determine your net worth. You are doing this for yourself, so don't be embarrassed if it's in a bad position right now. Simply add up the total current value of your assets and liabilities and subtract the total value of the liabilities from the total value of your assets. This is your net worth. If you can compare the value of each asset now to the value it had at the beginning of the year; you can also calculate the change in your net worth in percentage terms.

Are You Ready to Invest?

If you are debt-free or have a plan in place to take care of your debts and to build an emergency fund, you are ready to begin investing. The first rule of investing is to never invest more than you can afford to lose. If you go about your investment plan carefully, the chances of losing everything are slim to none. That said it's a wise approach to invest as if that could really happen. So, you shouldn't be investing next month's house payment or your kid's college funds in the hopes of gaining returns. After you have taken care of your debts and emergency fund, add up all of your basic living expenses, so you know how much you actually need per month. Anything left over above that is the amount of money you can invest for now.

Determining Your Financial Goals

Once you are in a position to invest something — even if you can only put in $100 a month now because you're paying off large debts — it's time to sit down and figure out your financial goals. There are several things to keep in mind:

Age: Generally speaking, the older you are, the more conservative you should be in your investment approach. The reason for this is simple. When things go badly, it takes time to recover and get back on the road to profitability. The older you are, the less time you have to grow your wealth in the future. That means a market crash, or a bad investment has larger consequences than it would have if you had thirty years to recover. Financial advisors generally recommend that older investors put their money in safer investments, which means putting some money into bonds and safe investments like US Treasuries that preserve capital. In the stock market, the older investor will seek out more stable companies that are larger, and while they may be growing, they have slow and steady growth with lower levels of risk. Of course, age can cut both ways. Many people reach their fifties with little to no savings or investment. If that describes your situation, you're going to want to invest more aggressively to seek rapid growth. Younger people also want to invest more aggressively, as they have a time horizon that permits taking on more risk. But time horizon isn't the only factor if you have no capital to protect; you definitely want to be more aggressive.

Chapter 3. Risks in Investing in Stocks

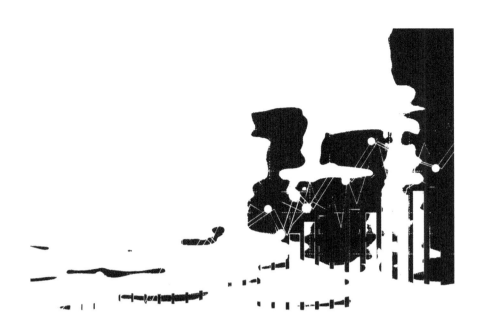

Understanding risk and volatility are two of the most important things to keep in mind with the stock market.

There are many different types of risk in the stock market. Some are direct, such as a small company that has the *potential* to make gains because of innovative products. Others are indirect and external. You can't manage all types of risks. Some come out of the blue, like the 9/11 terrorist attacks or the 2008 financial crash. So, if you think that you can control every form of risk, take a deep breath and realize you can't. In this chapter, we are going to try and describe every major category of risk investor's face, and if possible, we'll suggest ways to deal with them.

Emotional and Person Risk

First and foremost, you can control the risks to your investments that come from personal factors. These include fear, impatience, and greed. Emotions like these can be hard to control, but learning to take charge of them is essential if you are going to be a successful investor.

When real money is on the line, these emotions can become strong and overpowering. You must not let that happen.

The most common problem when it comes to emotions and personal risk is fear. When a stock market starts looking bearish, many investors immediately jump ship. They are making a huge mistake. A good investor is not getting in and out of the market at the slightest sign of a problem. In fact, selling off when everyone else is could be one of the biggest mistakes individual investors make. By the way, that doesn't exempt large investors. Many professional traders are subject to the same emotions and exhibit the same behavior during downturns. Massive selloffs are what cause bear markets to develop.

First of all, remember that you are looking to hold your investments over the long term. So, the ups and downs of the market and even recessions are not a reason to sell them. Over the past 50 years, by far the worst stock market contraction happened in the 2008 financial crisis. However, even that was short-lived. People that sold off their investments were either faced with being out of the markets altogether or having to get back in the markets when prices were appreciating. The lifetimes of other major bear markets were similar or even more short-lived. The first lesson in managing personal risk is to hold your investments through downturns.

The second lesson is that rather than giving into fear, you should start to see market downturns as opportunities. When prices are rapidly dropping due to a market sell-off, you should be buying shares. It's impossible to know where the bottom of a market is, and you shouldn't concern yourself with that.

At any time that share prices are declining, it's an opportunity, and so you should be making regular stock purchases. In one year, two years, or five years down the road, on average, the stocks that you purchased in a downturn are going to be worth quite a bit more.

The second problem that arises as a part of personal risk is greed. Many people start seeing dollar signs when they begin investing. Having a get-rich-quick mentality is not compatible with successful investing. Your approach should be centered on slowly and steadily accumulating wealth and not making a quick buck. As you invest, you're going to be coming across claims that certain trades or stocks are the next best thing, but you're better off ignoring such claims. More often than not, they turn out to be false. The stock market is not a gambling casino, even though many people treat it that way. You can avoid succumbing to greed by maintaining a regular investment program and not being taken in by the temptation that you can profit from short-term swings or "penny stocks" that are going to supposedly take off.

Finally, there is the related problem of impatience. After the Great Depression, people developed a more reasonable and cautious approach to the stock market. They realized that you're not going to get rich in six months or a year. The idea of long-term investing became dominant.

Unfortunately, in recent years, this lesson seems to be getting lost. More people are behaving like traders rather than as investors. Far too many investors are being taken in by the seduction of being able to beat market returns. Instead of being impatient, you should realize that you're in it for the long haul. Rather than trying to make a few extra bucks now, you're seeking to build wealth.

Risk of Loss of Capital

Obviously, financial risk is something you face when investing. Theoretically, there is a chance that you will lose all the money you invest in the stock market. This can happen if you tie your fate to a small number of companies. Several well-known companies like Lumber Liquidators, Bear-Stearns, and GM have either had major problems or gone completely under. Investors may have lost large sums in the process. The way to deal with this is to avoid investing in a small number of companies. Later in the chapter, we will investigate diversification as an investment strategy.

You'll also want to pay attention to the types of companies you invest in. Putting all of your money into small-cap stocks, for example, is probably a bad idea. So is putting all of your money into emerging markets, or into one sector of the stock market. Again, the key message is diversification. It's the way to protect you from financial risk.

Market and Economic Risk

Some factors are beyond your control, and the economy inevitably cycles through slowdowns and downturns. The market will cycle along with the economy, and also experience crashes when the economy may be doing fine overall. This happened in 1987, for example.

While these factors are not under your control, how you react to them is under your control. As we discussed in the section on emotional risk, you should not panic when there is a downturn. Remain level-headed, and use downturns as a buying opportunity. They are always followed by a brighter day; your job is to have the patience to wait for it to arrive.

Interest Rate Risk

Changing interest rates can impact the markets. Although this is a book about stock market investing, you should have some awareness of how bond markets work. You should also be aware that investor money can flow back and forth between bond and stock markets depending on conditions.

One thing that bond markets offer is the safety of capital, especially when we are talking about U.S. government bonds. When interest rates are high, U.S. government bonds (and other types of bonds, including corporate and municipal bonds) become very attractive.

Interest rate changes have risks for bond investors, however. Bonds are traded on secondary markets. When interest rates rise, bond prices fall because older bonds that offer lower interest rates become less attractive. Conversely, when interest rates fall, older bonds that pay higher interest rates have more value than new bonds being issued that pay relatively low rates.

This doesn't directly affect a stock market investor, but if demand for bonds rises, that can mean less capital flowing into the stock market. Less demand means lower prices, so the market may see declines.

Also, as we'll see, you can invest in bonds through the stock market using exchange-traded funds. If you are using this method, you'll want to keep close tabs on interest rates. That means paying closer attention to the Federal Reserve and its quarterly announcements. You should be doing so even if you are not going to invest in bonds in any way.

Announcements on interest rate changes can have a large impact on stock prices. But as always, keep your eye on the long ball. If the markets react negatively to an increase in interest rates that can be an opportunity to buy undervalued stocks.

Political Risk and Government

Government and politics can create big risks in the stock market. International events can cause market crashes, and these days even a tweet from the President can cause markets to rise and fall. Lately, some politicians have also been discussing breaking up the big tech companies. Others are talking about investigating them. Such talk — and worse actions— can have a negative impact on the markets. Part of your job as an investor is to keep a close eye on the news. You're going to want to know what's happening so that you can adjust if necessary.

Inflation Risk

Inflation hasn't been high in decades. However, in the late 1970s inflation rates were routinely in the double digits. Hopefully, that isn't going to be something that happens anytime soon, because high inflation rates can eat your returns alive. If the stock market is appreciating at 7% per year, but inflation is 14%, you can see that it's like having debt but investing in stocks — it's a losing proposition. Right now, inflation risk is very low, but you'll want to have some awareness of it and always keep tabs on it. High inflation rates also tend to go hand-in-hand with high interest rates, since the Federal Reserve will raise rates to try and slow down inflation. That means that bonds might become more attractive when inflation gets out of control.

Taxes and Commissions

Finally, we have the risk imposed by taxes. Of course, we are all going to be hit with taxes no matter where our money comes from. However, you need to take into account the taxes that you are going to pay when it comes to any gains you realize on the stock market. Part of being a successful investor is having an understanding of how much your taxes are cutting into your profits. If you are investing for the long-term, it will be less of an issue. But keep in mind that taxes can really eat into short-term trades. Frequent, short-term traders also face risk from commissions and fees. If you execute a lot of trades, the commissions can add up. This is not an issue for long-term investors.

Risk vs. Return

One of the fundamental trade-offs that an investor will make is risk vs. return. Generally speaking, the higher the risk, the greater the *possibility* of good returns. In 1998, Amazon was a pretty high-risk investment. While it had potential, major bookstores like Borders and Barnes & Noble dominated the space. Amazon was on shaky ground at the time, and another company could have come in and competed successfully for online book sales. That never happened, and Amazon ended up dominating book sales and expanding widely across retail and into cloud computing. That risk has translated into massive returns. A $10,000 investment in 1998 would be worth more than $1 million today.

But hindsight is 20/20. Today, there are similar opportunities all around us, but it's hard to know which ones will end up being successful over the long term. If you are an aggressive investor, part of your job will be estimating which companies are the best bets for the future.

These examples serve to illustrate why a diversified portfolio is essential.

Managing Risk

There are a few time-tested strategies that have been developed that help manage risk. They even minimize, as much as possible, the kinds of risk that you will face that are completely out of control. That could include anything from a terrorist attack to interest rate changes.

These strategies are simple and easy to understand. The problem is that in practice, many investors fail to follow them, and instead let their decision-making be guided by emotions. You might end up following that path as well. However, we are going to give you the tools you need to avoid it. It's up to you whether you utilize them or not.

Chapter 4. How to Invest in Stocks
(How to Buy Your First Stock)

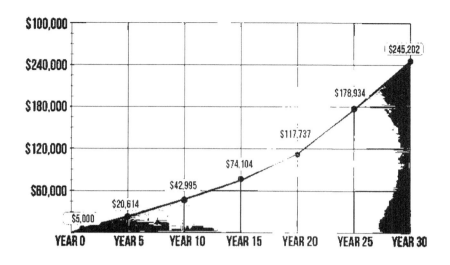

How to Get Start

Stock may seem incredibly intimidating for those starting in the investment world. It looks like a completely different world, and the hardest step for most is the beginning. However, it is quite simple to get started in stock investments. First, one must set goals for themselves and determine how they would like to invest in a stock. By writing down goals and ensuring that the investor's money is used in the best possible way, the investor is helping them yield the highest return on their investment. Once the individual's goals are made clear, they must plan on how to meet those goals. After this, they may choose the best investment method for achieving these goals. Then, it must be decided on where exactly the investor will go to invest their money. It is crucial, as this will be the platform by which the investor will trade their stocks. After this, the investor must open an account with whomever they choose. Before they start trading, the investor must make an initial investment using this account. While doing so, they may have to link their bank account to their stock trading account. The investor must then begin the process of buying and selling stocks using this account. Although this seems like a lengthy process, it is quite simple.

Planning and Meeting Goals

Investors must familiarize themselves with their goals. It is quite helpful to write down one's goals in each area and put them somewhere that is easily accessible. It is useful to have measurable goals to reach. This way, there may be a specific period and amount that may be assigned to the targets. It may help to come up with monthly goals. For instance, the investor may start with the purchase of 100 shares of stock in February. They may wish to increase that to 150 shares by March, 200 shares by April, and so on. This way, the investor may have a period to achieve their goals. It will allow them to measure their progress easily.

To set proper goals, one must reflect upon their past. How much will the investor be able to set aside for stock realistically? If one's goals are not realistic, it may become discouraging and set the investor back from their full potential. The investor must consider any past investments they have made. They must consider what worked and what did not. It is crucial to consider income and expenses when investing, and one must also consider any savings goals that one has. This will make it more apparent what may be invested in stocks.

Without a clear guide on how to invest, the investor will lack direction. It may lead to spur-of-the-moment decisions, and the investor may regret these choices. There may be some periods where one will not trade, as it won't be as profitable. Perhaps the market is down, and the trader does not wish to sell any stock. Perhaps the market is up, and the trader does not want to buy any stock. There will be events such as vacations, holidays, stressful events, or emergencies.

One must also consider how much money they have. Although it is possible to double one's money in a year, it is not likely for a beginner to do so. One may also choose to invest one time and hold it, or they may choose to invest more into their account often. This time and amount will depend on the investor and their financial situation.

The investor must also choose a strategy. They may wish to buy and sell stocks or to buy and hold stocks. They may even consider options trading. Whichever method that the investor chooses, there will be different goals to fit those strategies.

Long-term goals may be set to help the investor. Although planning for the following year may help the investor, longer periods may prove even more beneficial. Perhaps the investor wishes to acquire a million dollars worth of stock in the succeeding ten years. Perhaps the investor wishes to save a certain amount for retirement, which they wish to have by the next 25 years. Whatever the end goal is, the investor must make that clear so that they can begin working towards it immediately. Once a proper plan is created for meeting the investor's goals, they may move to the next step.

Choosing an Investment Method

After the investor has set goals and created a plan to meet them, it is time to decide on which investment method they wish to pursue. For those that wish to trade on their own completely, the DIY (do-it-yourself) method is the best fit. The investor may conduct all their trades online, making transfers from the bank manually or automatically. It will allow full control of one's investments. There will also be complete independence over what the investor wishes to buy and sell, how much they wish to trade, and how often they wish to trade.

They will, however, need to dedicate time to researching, making any transfers, trading, and other procedures. There is also a higher risk for this choice, as a beginning investor will not have the education that a financial advisor will. They also won't be under the control of a Robo-Advisor. However, all the profit that is made by the investor will be theirs to keep. They won't have to pay commission and fees outside of any required by the broker that they use.

The least independent approach to investing in stock is by hiring a financial advisor. It is for those who do not wish to touch their stock at all and to have it fully regulated for them. Hesitant beginners may benefit from this method. It is important to remember, however, that this method tends to be the costliest. It is most beneficial for those with higher assets and larger portfolios. It is also important to choose an investor that will work to meet the investor's goals, not just the goals of themselves. Therefore, the investor must set specific goals for themselves and how they wish to invest their money. They may more easily communicate with the advisor their desires, which may be carried out for them.

Choosing a Stockbroker

When investing for oneself, a proper stockbroker must be chosen. This will depend on the individual's needs and wants. For some, their bank that they already operate offers stock investments through their bank. This is a quick and simple option, as their money will already be linked through the bank, and they may already be familiar with their style. There may also be options for financial advisors in the bank that are free of charge. Otherwise, the investor must research their options before settling on a broker.

When choosing a stockbroker, the investor should research any fees (transaction fees, maintenance fees, etc.), minimum funds required to open an account, any commission collected by the stockbroker, and accessibility. The investor may prefer a specific type of formatting for their broker to have. There may also be free education, customer service, and other ways to make investing easier for the investor.

The investor must choose the option that will allow them to make the highest return on their investments. The investor should keep in mind which services they are likely to use most frequently, and they should choose the broker that charges the least to use those services. There may be transactional fees, which are costs for buying and selling stocks. Many beginning investors tend to forget this, so it is essential to take this into account.

Opening an Account

When opening an account, there are often a few steps that are required. This is typically not a lengthy process, but the investor should be aware of the potential actions associated with opening an account.

The first step when opening an online account is typically to create an account. This will consist of a username and password, as well as some personal information. This may include setting goals, determining which types of features the investor wishes to use, and the investor's experience level. This information will help to create the optimal experience for the investor.

There may also be an application for the account to ensure that the investor is qualified to hold the account. There may also be an agreement stating that the investor assumes all the risks of investing and understands that the money is not insured or guaranteed. Initial Investment and Linking Accounts

During the application process, the investor will most likely be prompted to fund the account. This can be done in several ways. The investor may transfer the funds electronically via an EFT (Electronic funds transfer). This is transferring the money from a linked bank account and will most likely only take one business day to transfer. The investor may also choose to make a wire transfer, which is a transfer directly from the bank. It is important to consider how much to invest in the account initially carefully. For those just starting, there may not be much money to invest at first. The minimum investment amounts for the broker should be looked over beforehand.

Buying and Selling Stocks

After the investor funds their account, it is time to start trading the stocks. It must be decided what stock, how much of the stock, and how the investor wishes to buy. Once these factors are decided, the investor must buy the stock. It is usually as simple as searching the stock symbol and selecting "buy." It is best to wait until the stock is at a low, but the investor must also begin investing as early as possible in experiencing the benefits of investing. When the stock is bought, it will typically take a bit to process and for the broker to receive these funds. After that, it will show up in the online portfolio of the investor. When it is time to sell this stock, the investor may typically visit their portfolio and click "sell" on the desired stock.

Chapter 5. When to Buy and Sell Stock

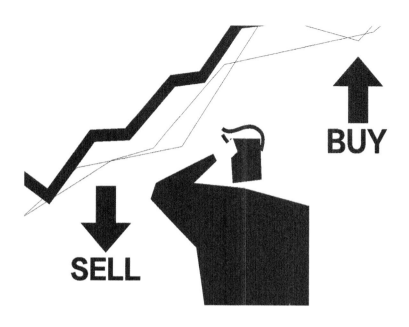

When to Sell a Stock

Determining when to sell a stock is a decision that even the world's best investors wrestle with. Warren Buffett has said that his holding period for a stock is forever. Does Buffett really hold every stock that he buys forever? Of course not! The point that he is making is that you should always purchase a stock with the intention of holding it forever; therefore, make sure your money has been put into your best investment ideas. An investor should leave his or her portfolio intact for at least five years, as long as the fundamentals for which a particular stock was purchased do not deteriorate. Investors should pay no attention to a stock's price volatility because it is a normal part of the investment cycle. As a long-term investor, there will be times when it makes sense to sell or reduce your position in stock earlier than you had planned. Next, we will talk about different circumstances in which you should consider selling a stock or reducing your position in a stock.

- **The Time Frame** — If you need the money within five years, it should not be invested in stocks. It would be best to invest your money in safe and stable short-term instruments. Money market accounts, money market funds, and short-term certificates of deposits would be better options. Since the Great Recession struck, some investment professionals now recommend that you not invest any money in stocks that will be needed within 10 years.

- **An Overvalued Stock** — When a stock is significantly overvalued, sell it. Take the proceeds from the sale and invest them into other undervalued stocks that you have researched. The P/E ratio is still one of the best indicators of value. For example, if a stock has traded at an average P/E of 15 for the last seven to 10 years and the business is thriving, but the stock currently trades at a P/E of 30 or more on consistent or increasing EPS, you should seriously consider selling the stock. The PEG ratio is also a very effective method for determining if a stock is now overvalued.
- **Too Much Debt** — Too much debt is dangerous for any business because there's always the chance that a business may be unable to pay its debt. Too much

debt also puts a business at greater risk of failure if a downturn in the industry or economy were to occur. Upon entering the 2007 recession, thousands of businesses here in the United States literally disappeared overnight and that was before things really got bad.

- **Too Much Risk** — You have already learned the importance of staying away from investments that are too risky. Sometimes new management will come to a business and begin to implement new policies; along with that implementation, they will knowingly or unknowingly expose a business to greater risk. If you purchased the stock of a business that stayed away from very risky practices, but the business has now begun to display risky behaviors that make you uncomfortable, sell the stock and find yourself a better investment.

- **Loss of Competitive Advantage** — You have also learned that we should only be purchasing the stocks of businesses that have a durable competitive advantage. When a business changes its business model, resulting in it losing its competitive advantage, sell the stock.

- **The Portfolio Lacks Balance or Diversification** — It's very easy for your best performing stock to become the largest holding in your portfolio, and there's absolutely nothing wrong with that. The problem arises when the stock makes up more than 20-25% of your portfolio's total value. Legendary investor, Jim Slater suggests that individual investors limit the number of funds invested in a single stock within their portfolios to a maximum of 15%. When your portfolio becomes heavily weighted in one stock, consider reducing your position of that stock to bring more balance and better diversification into your portfolio.
- **Stock Reaches Its Fair Value** — Our goal as investors should always be to purchase a stock at a discount to its fair value and it is recommended at least a 25% discount to its fair value. By doing so, when you sell a stock that has reached its fair value, you are guaranteed a gain of at least 25% from the sale. This is a disciplined approach to selling a stock.

According to research, it was common for Benjamin Graham to sell a stock once it had a 50% gain in price. If the future prospects of a particular stock look good, you may decide to sell only a portion of the stock, such as half of its shares, and hold on to the rest when using this approach.

- **When Your Analysis is Found to Be Flawed**— There will be times when an investor will be very detailed and careful in his or her analysis of a particular company or its stock, only to find out later that his or her analysis is incorrect or flawed. Whether a stock should be sold at that time depends on the seriousness of the error and its impact on the long-term performance of the business. So, when you find that you have incorrectly analyzed a particular business, it is essential for you to take a serious look at all available information to determine whether or not to sell the stock or to continue holding it. One thing is certain, as an investor, you will not always be right when analyzing a company or its stock.

There is no clear-cut way to determine the optimal time to sell a stock. There will be times that you will sell a stock because it has not performed well, only to see it skyrocket and double or triple in price soon after you sell it. There will also be occasions when you have purchased what seems to be the perfect stock, only to watch it tumble in price and for no apparent reason. Learn what you can from these events and move on. Even Peter Lynch, Jim Slater, and other great investors have sold stocks too early or too late. It's going to happen sometimes.

When to Buy a Stock

After the investor funds their account, it is time to start trading the stocks. It must be decided what stock, how much of the stock, and how the investor wishes to buy. Once these factors are decided, the investor must buy the stock. It is usually as simple as searching the stock symbol and selecting "buy." It is best to wait until the stock is at a low, but the investor must also begin investing as early as possible in experiencing the benefits of investing. When the stock is bought, it will typically take a bit to process and for the broker to receive these funds. After that, it will show up in the online portfolio of the investor. When it is time to sell this stock, the investor may typically visit their portfolio and click "sell" on the desired stock.

Starting out as a stock investor is quite simple. The investor must follow a few steps to become a stock trader. They must choose an investment method, select a stockbroker, open an account, a fund that account, and they will be ready to go.

Your very first stock trade can be frightening - not to mention confounding. You've done your stock research, you believe you've found a winner, and now you're all set to put your brand-new brokerage account to excellent usage and begin trading — nevertheless, you're not quite sure how to "carry it out."

Trade "execution" is just an elegant technique for describing an exchange. To "trade" typically describes a particular kind of investing method, so certifying your use of the term "trade" with "carry out" lets other financiers understand that you're going over a particular exchange.

The real-time it takes to perform your trade can move from broker to broker and market to market. (The SEC requires that all brokerage companies supply documents quarterly to the basic population about the handling of their customer orders).

Your broker will unquestionably put your order through their complicated trading computer system network to get a hold of your shares when you do put in your order. In many cases, your order will never ever leave the broker — your brokerage company ought to clean out shares of the organization you're purchasing from its stock.

You have a couple of choices when it comes to trading stocks beyond merely selling and purchasing. Basically, you get shares of a particular stock and sell them, relying on that the stock will diminish in worth, leaving the distinction between the selling rate and ultimate repurchase rate in your pocket.

Stock Order Types

Naturally, buying stocks is similarly more complex than only one purchase. There are numerous different approaches for considering your purchase, all going concerning cost, the time point of confinement, which is simply the start.

Anyhow, what are your alternatives for purchasing stock? There are 5 various types of stock orders that your broker will likely let you utilize.

A market order is a demand to sell a stock or buy at the existing market value. Market orders are quite a great deal for the basic stock order, and because the capability is typically performed instantly.

Something to keep as a primary top priority with a market order is the way you do not manage the amount you pay for your stock purchase or sale; the marketplace does.

The speed with which online market orders have actually launched might have made this less of a danger than it used to be. The market still moves quicker.

Some individuals do not have problems with this, for those that do this, imperfection can be met with a breaking point order.

- **Point of Confinement Order**

A breaking point order can keep you from purchasing or selling your stock at a rate that you do not want, possibly assisting you in keeping a strategic range from a horrible choice. On the off possibility that the cost is a misdirected base and not in tune with the market, nevertheless, the order will never ever be made.

Keep in mind that some brokers charge more for point of confinement orders, as the trade might not go through.

- **Stop-loss Order**

Stop-loss orders, when that price is reached, transform into market orders. The target price is hit, and the trade is executed at market value.

- **Stop-Limit Order**

Stop-limit orders are also stopped orders based on hanging tight at a particular expense. Stop-limit orders end up being point of confinement orders when the target cost is reached as opposed to market orders.

Changing into a breaking point order can be something useful for a stop order, staying away from particular threats. On the occasion that the shares topple to $20.00 at the very same time, then instantly shoot back up, your market order might go through in any case.

- **Tracking Stop**

Generally, this is a stop order based upon a portion modification in the market cost instead of setting a target cost.

You can pick to what degree the order stays open when you put an order into your broker. Naturally, orders are day orders, indicating that they are signed up until completion of the trading day. Outstanding till-canceled orders stay open until you really enter and cancel them.

Chapter 6. How to Generate Passive Income from the Stock Market

Income investing is a little bit of a different ballgame than growth investing. In this case, we are seeking out companies that pay dividends. That means ignoring a lot of high growth stocks like Amazon and Netflix. It also means ignoring disruptive companies with potential like Tesla. When you are an income investor, you are looking to make a certain level of income from your stock holdings. That may be now, or it may be in the future. But your portfolio is going to look quite different from a growth investor, and even a value-oriented growth investor.

Yield

Start compiling a diverse list of companies that pay dividends that you find interesting. In each case, track the yield, which is the dividend divided by the share price. That will help you compare apples-to-apples when judging one dividend stock against another. Keep in mind that you are going to be seeking some kind of balance, so buying up stocks with the highest yields isn't the best philosophy. To see why to consider a company called consolidated communications. They pay a yield of 32%. The problem is, it's a penny stock. That means it's only $4 or so a share.

Most analysts are rating it a SELL. A glance at the chart indicates it has dropped from a $29 share price over the past couple of years, and yet it's still rated as being overvalued. These are major red flags.

Dividend

You may also be interested in the actual dividend payment, and not just the yield. IBM pays $6 a share, but Apple only pays $1.55 a share. So, you'd have to own more than three Apple shares for every share of IBM you could buy in order to get the same annual income from your stocks. Since IBM is cheaper on a per-share basis, that is something to take into consideration.

Dividend Growth

For any stock that you invest in, you're going to want to look at the history of their dividend payments. The ideal dividend stock is one that pays higher dividends over time. IBM is a great example because they paid consistent dividends through the 2008 financial crisis, and they have been increasing their dividends since then. Dividend growth ensures that your dividend payments will keep up with or exceed inflation.

DRIPS and Reinvesting

If you have a large amount of capital available right now, you can buy up shares of stock and start living off the dividend payments. However, if you are looking at a long-term investment program, you are going to want to reinvest your dividends. In the future, you're going to want to have as many shares as possible, so taking cash out now simply doesn't make sense. Instead, the payments from dividends should be used to purchase additional shares. Some companies even allow you to purchase fractional shares with the money.

A DRIP is a Dividend Reinvestment Program. In this case, the company will automatically take any dividends you earn and use them to buy additional shares. This will help enforce discipline in case you get tempted to cash out your dividends and waste the money on a trip or new car. Instead, the company will force you to save for the future.

Exchange-Traded Funds

The possibility of using exchange-traded funds to meet your investment goals always exists. In this case, you can seek out an ETF that invests in dividend stocks. You will still receive dividend payments, and the fund will have built-in diversification. When looking at ETFs to use for dividend investing, be sure to focus on yield, and pick funds that have the highest yields. Many investors can do a mixture of both; you could invest in ETFs while also investing in specific companies like IBM.

Alternative Investments

The world of dividend investing isn't restricted to traditional stock investing. You can also invest in the following:

- REITS
- MLPs
- BDCs

A REIT is a real estate trust. This is a company that owns hard property assets and rents them out. The types of property are quite varied. For example, you can invest in

REITs that own rental homes, apartments, or commercial real estate. There are also REITs that own hotels and resorts. In fact, any type of property that you can think of is represented by at least one REIT. But interestingly, there are REITs that have great prospects for the future because they are technology-related. For example, some REITs own cell phone towers, and there are others that own cloud computing.

REITs pay high dividends, and they trade like stocks on the stock market. Investing in REITs is a good way to get some exposure to real estate and other types of property ownership.

An MLP is a master limited partnership. These companies are midstream energy companies that transport oil and gas, own pipelines, or own refinement facilities. These are great investments to consider, and they also pay high dividends. You also invest in them by purchasing shares on the stock market. These types of investments are particularly noteworthy because the companies are partnerships and not corporations. When you invest, you become a limited partner. This means that you can deduct company expenses on your tax returns. Essentially, a large share of the income from an MLP is tax-free.

The final alternative investment that we are looking at is called a BDC, or Business Development Corporation. They also trade on stock exchanges and pay dividends. These are financial companies that invest in small to mid-sized companies that need cash. They can provide loans to companies or take an ownership stake.

When to Cash Out

Cashing out is a personal decision. By cashing out, in this case, we don't mean selling off your shares. What we mean is when should you stop reinvesting and start taking dividends as cash income. The answer is you start doing this when the level of dividend payments you receive starts matching your desired income.

Don't be afraid to shake up your portfolio. If you find an investment that suits your needs better than stocks you are currently invested in, then you should be ready to sell some of your shares and invest in the other stock. There is no reason for you to be locked into a particular stock, you can buy shares in other companies and then start getting dividend payments from them in the next upcoming cycle.

Fundamentals Always Matter

No matter which path you choose, when dividend investing, you want to pay close attention to the fundamentals. In the end, fundamentals are what matters. A company with good fundamentals is going to be a good investment. So, you'll want some trade-off between solid fundamentals, yield, and dividend payment that suits your goals. Remember to always think long-term.

Bond Investing

Finally, if you are looking for an income investing portfolio, consider buying exchange-traded funds that invest in bonds.

As we discussed earlier, there is a wide array of choices, allowing you to find the right amount of risk and the right interest payments. You'll want to look at the yields of the bond funds. Some have high rates of growth and high yields. That is, you can achieve growth as well as income by investing in bond funds too. The advantage of using ETFs is that you can avoid the hassle of trying to invest in bond markets.

Chapter 7. The Main Mistakes of a Beginner

Mistakes happen in every field, sector, and industry. Some are always anticipated, while others happened unexpectedly. When it comes to stock trading, there are several mistakes that you can make. Understanding these mistakes can help you avoid them, thus ending up successful in your stock investments. Here are some of the common mistakes made by most investors, beginners, and professional traders alike:

Failure to Understand the Trade

It is always wrong to invest in a trade or business you know nothing about. It is a great mistake to engage in stock trading when you do not understand the business and financial models involved. You can avoid this mistake by taking the time to research the stock market and stock trading before investing your money. Know the different markets, the driving forces, as well as trading procedures.

Most investors tend to buy stocks from the latest companies and industries they know very little about. Although such companies may look promising, it is difficult to determine whether they will continue to exist. Understanding a specific company gives you a better hand over other investors. You will be able to make accurate predictions about the company or industry, which may bring you more profit. You will quickly tell when the business is booming, stagnating, or closing way before other investors get this information.

Individuals who do not take time to study companies miss out on future trends of these companies. Failing to establish such trends leads to several missed opportunities. For instance, a person who invests in a company that is higher than his capital may quickly lose all his investment. That is why it is always advisable that you invest in the industry you understand better. For instance, if you are a surgeon, you can invest in stocks that deal with medicine or related stocks. Lawyers can invest in companies that generate income through litigation, and so on.

Impatience

The stock market is for patient investors. It is a slow but steady form of investment. Although it bears various opportunities that can bring you money, you cannot make enough profit in one day. Most stock investors are always faced with the challenge of being patient. Some end up losing trade positions before they mature in the quest to make quick money. Exiting the market too early will always cost you some returns. As a new investor, you must never expect your investment portfolio to perform more than its capability, as this will always lead to a disaster. Remain realistic in terms of the time, duration, and resources needed to earn from the market.

Failure to Diversify

Another mistake that easily causes disaster is the failure to diversify. Professional investors do not have a problem with this since they can easily profit from a single type of stock. However, young investors must be able to diversify to secure their investment. Some of them do not stick to this principle. Most of these lose a great fortune as soon as they get onto the stock market. As you seek to invest, remember the rule of thumb governing stock diversity. This states that you should not invest more than 10% of your capital in one type of stock.

Getting Too Connected with a Certain Company

The essence of trading in stock is to make a profit. Sometimes, investors get too deep into a certain company that they forget that it is all about the shares and not the company itself. Being too attached to a company may cloud your judgment when it comes to stock trading since you may end up buying stocks from this company instead of getting the best deal on the market. As you learn more about companies, always remember that you are into the business to make money, besides creating relationships.

Investment Turnover

Investment turnover refers to the act of entering and exiting positions at will. This is one other mistake that destroys great investments. It is only beneficial to institutions that seek to benefit from low commission rates. Most stock trading positions charge transaction fees. The more frequently you buy and sell, the more you pay in terms of transaction fees. You, therefore, need to be careful when entering positions. Do not get in or exit too early. Have a rough idea of when you want to close positions so that you do not miss some of the long-term benefits of these positions.

Timing the Market

Market timing results in high investment turnover. It is not easy to successfully time the market. On average, only 94% of stock trading returns are acquired without the use of market timing. Most traders time the market as a way of attempting to recover their losses. They want to get even by making some profit to counter a loss. This is always known as a cognitive error in behavioral finance. Trying to get even on the stock market will always result in double losses.

Trading with Emotions

Allowing your emotions to rule is one of the things that kill your stock investment returns. Most people get into the market for fear of losses or thirst to make returns too fast. As a young trader, you must ensure that greed and fear do not overwhelm your decision-making. Stock prices may fluctuate a lot in the short-term; however, this may not be the case in the long term, especially for large-cap stocks.

This means that you may get lower profits in the short term, but these may increase in the long term. Understanding this will help you avoid closing trades when it is not the right time yet.

Setting Unrealistic Expectations

This always occurs when dealing with small-cap stocks such as penny stocks. Most investors buy such stocks with the expectation that the prices will change drastically. Sometimes this works, but it is not a guarantee. To make great fortunes, people invest a lot of capital in these stocks, and then the prices do not change much. If these investors are not prepared for such an eventuality, they may feel frustrated and may quit the business completely. However, this is something that you must be able to manage if you want to grow your investment. Do not expect more than what a certain type of stock can deliver.

Using Borrowed Money

This is probably one of the greatest mistakes that investors make. Some investors get carried away with the returns they are making. As a way of getting more profits, they borrow money and use it to enter more stock positions. This is a very dangerous move and can result in a lot of stress. Stock trading is like gambling. You are not always sure how much you take home at the end of each trade. It is therefore not advisable for you to invest borrowed money in it.

As you try to avoid these mistakes, you must also avoid getting information from the wrong sources. Some traders have lost a fortune because they relied on the wrong sources for stock information. It is important to isolate a small number of people and places where you will seek guidance from. Do not be a person that follows the crowd. Take time before investing in new stock opportunities. Carry out proper due diligence, especially with small-cap stocks since these involve a lot of risks. Remember, you must trade carefully and implement expert advice if you want to succeed in stock trading.

CRASH COURSE

Chapter 8. Insider Tricks Used by Professional Traders

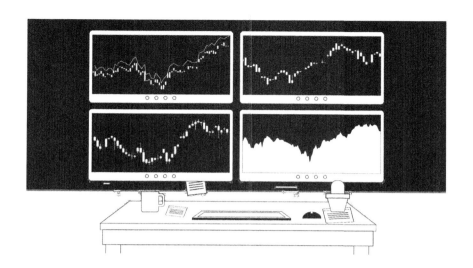

An investor should always be on the lookout for signals that might be clues about their investments. One signal you should be keeping an eye on is the actions taken by the insiders with a company. Are they sticking by the company and investing in it? Or do they seem to be running away from it despite amazing stock prices? These can be important clues as to the health and intermediate future of the company. One thing you need to keep tabs on is whether or not the insiders are buying or selling shares of the company. You'll also want to note major departures from the company. Of course, the company is going to make up some pleasant story about why some major figure is leaving. You know, they want to spend more time with their grandmother. But is that really what's going on? If other news or more signals are indicating otherwise, including insider moves, you might view such news with a negative eye. People often leave a sinking ship.

Insider Trading

Here we aren't talking about criminal activity, but rather a company members themselves who own shares of the company that they are associated with. A good indication that people are confident in the future of their company is finding out that they own and are buying more shares of stock in their own company. On the other hand, if they are selling off their shares, that can be a sign that the people actually running the company or involved with it don't have that much confidence in its future.

It's actually possible to find out what company insiders are doing when it comes to shares of stock in their own company. The Securities and Exchange Commission requires them to file publicly available reports. You can find publicly filed reports on a government website known as "Edgar." It can be found here:

https://www.sec.gov/edgar.shtml

"Insiders" will file various forms, including an initial form that they have to submit to the government indicating their insider status with the company. This is called form 3.

If you are researching this data, you're going to want to pay special attention to form 4 and form 144. On form 4, any transactions involving a large number of shares are recorded. So, if the insider bought a large number of shares, it would be recorded on form 4. Also, if they sold a large number of shares, it's going to be reported on form 4.

If a single insider is selling shares, that doesn't necessarily mean anything. However, if you notice that multiple insiders are off-loading their shares, pay attention. That might be an indication that a large number of people who are in the know about the company's prospects aren't confident about the company's future.

Form 144 is related to a special class of stock called restricted stock. This is stock that the insider was provided as compensation for employment. If they decide to unload it after a required holding period, this will be noted with form 144.

In summary, if insiders are confident that the company is doing well and has solid long-term prospects, they are probably going to be buying shares in the company, not trying to get rid of them. You will want to take this kind of information and incorporate it into the larger picture of course. It's important to consider all the indicators for the company and not get lost in the details of focusing on one sign. So, if you notice that there is a large sell-off, you'll want to check other information like the company's latest earnings reports.

Quantity also Matters

Don't get alarmed if people sell a small number of shares. When they are trying to divest their own portfolio of any interest in the company, it is when you should take notice.

Congressional Insiders

A few years ago, the news program 60 Minutes did an interesting investigation. They found that members of Congress were playing the role of insiders at many companies and getting advantageous stock buys as a result. Unfortunately, there isn't much we can do about that, but it's good to have awareness about it.

Stock Buybacks

Stock buybacks can be a good sign or a bad sign. If a company is doing well, a stock buyback can be used as a way for a company to pass on profits to investors. However, stock buybacks can also be an indicator that a company is heading for trouble. The first thing to consider is that the company has lower than expected earnings. In that case, a company might use a stock buyback in order to artificially boost their indicators on the stock market. Buying back shares of stock, if done on a large enough scale, can alter important metrics like the price per earnings ratio and earnings per share. If you have fewer shares but the same earnings, earnings per share are going to look more favorable. They can do this in the hopes of artificially boosting the value of the stock and hence it's the market price. Consider an example. Suppose that a company has $500 in earnings and 100 shares. The earnings per share are $5. If they buy back 50 shares, then you still have $500 in earnings, but with 50 shares, so now the earnings per share are $10. That looks better to investors taking a cursory look at the stock, but in reality, the company's prospects haven't changed.

Another negative possibility is that the company has stagnated. If companies are out of ideas and not pursuing new ones, they aren't investing a large amount of money into research and development. That means they have cash sitting around and using a stock buyback could be a simple way to unload the cash.

You'll also want to check the price-to-earnings ratio and look up to see if the stock is overvalued. It can be a bad sign when a company is buying back overvalued shares.

Another question to ask is, where is the company getting the cash used for the buyback? Hopefully, they have enough money on hand to do it. But if they are borrowing money for the share buyback, that is definitely a sign that the company is unhealthy.

If you have invested in a company and they engage in a share buyback, you'll want to investigate further to find out what's behind it. In many cases, it's not something to worry about. However, sometimes it's an indicator that the future with this company is not so bright.

Stock Splits

Another corporate action you will need to be aware of is a stock split. Companies can do stock splits or reverse stock splits. In a stock split, a share is converted from 1 share to 2 or 3 or more shares. That immediately changes the price per share and impacts metrics like earnings per share. Imagine that a company has a share trading at $100, and it has 100 shares outstanding, and earnings per share of $5, meaning they have a price to earnings ratio of $20. If they do a 2-1 split, now there are 200 shares. The amount of money invested in the company hasn't changed, so the share price immediately drops to $50 a share. Now you have twice the number of shares in your portfolio, so the value of your investment hasn't changed. Earnings per share would be cut in half and would be reported as $2.50. The price-to-earnings ratio would remain at $20.

One reason a company might do a stock split is to reduce the price of a share, in order to attract more investors.

A stock trading at $1,000 a share might be unaffordable for a lot of small investors. If a company was interested in attracting more small investors, they might to a 4-1 stock split and drop the share price to $250 per share. A stock split for a high-priced stock can also increase liquidity. That is, it will increase the ease with which you can sell your shares. Very high-priced stocks will have large bid-ask spreads, which can make them harder to sell. Doing a split and bringing the price back down to a lower level can reduce the bid-ask spread and make it easier for investors to sell their shares.

A reverse stock split is going to reduce the number of shares that you own. So, if you own 100 shares and they did a 1-2 reverse split, you would only own 50 shares after that. If the share price had been $100, it would rise to $200 after the split. Remember that the amount of money invested remains the same before and after the split, so the share price also has to change if the number of shares changes.

Chapter 9. Tips and Tricks for Successful Stocks Trading

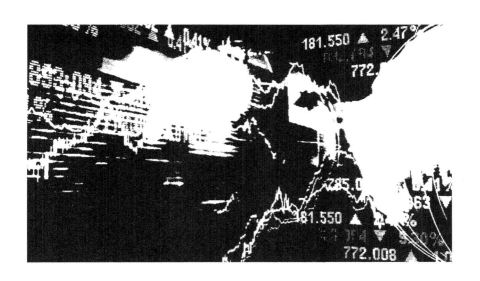

There are some tips and tricks that you can keep up your sleeve to help you invest in stocks. Let us look at some of them.

Always Be Informed

You need to be informed about what happens in the market. This is the only way you can trust your decisions. You should go through different resources and publications if you want to obtain more information about the various stocks in the market.

Buy Low, Sell High

This is a strategy that most investors will use. It is always good to buy low and sell high, and you must follow this to the tee. It is when you do this that you can expect to make large profits in the market. When you buy low and sell high, you will purchase a stock at its lowest value and sell it at its highest value. It will be easy for you to determine when the stock price will reach the highest rate based on some methods and data you collect. You need to ensure that you always act according to the data that you have collected. Experts recommend that it is a good idea to buy stocks the minute the market opens. Most stocks reach their highest price in the afternoon, and that is when you should sell them.

Scalping

This is a very popular technique in the stock market. When you use this technique, you can always buy and sell stocks within a matter of a few seconds. Your purchases and sales depend on how fast you are. This is a very strange method, but it is very effective, especially in volatile markets. Let us assume that you purchased a stock at 10:00 A.M. and sold it at 10:02 A.M. The price of that stock is $3, and the selling price is $5. So, in a matter of two minutes, you made a $2 profit per share, and this is a great profit for a scalper. This does not seem like a profit, but if you do this at least twenty or thirty times a day, you can make a huge profit. You should only use this form of trading once you have enough experience in the market. If you want to take up this technique, you should have at least a year's worth of experience to help you make the right decisions.

Short Selling

Many traders use the concept of short selling when they invest in the market. Short selling refers to when you need to borrow stock from the holder and sell it to another buyer. Then, you will wait for the stock price to fall before you give the stocks back to the lender. This is one of the easiest ways in which you can capitalize on the volatility of the prices. You must make the right decisions about the investments you make and not invest or borrow useless stocks. You must always ensure that you maintain a wide margin that will make a few mistakes. You should ensure that you have enough capital to support any other investments if things never work out. It is always good to buy shares back at the earliest if you believe that the price of the stocks will continue to increase.

Identify the Pattern

It is important to remember that stocks and every other stock in the market will follow a pattern. Once you notice this pattern and understand it, you can invest in stocks successfully. This pattern has all the information you need about the high and low points of the stocks and gathers some information on how you can trade between those points. It is important to have the history of the stock with you since it will help you determine the previous trend and predict the future trend of the stock.

Look at the Results

Every company is result-oriented, which means that the report published by the company will tell you how well the company is doing. The report that the company shares will shed some light on how well it is doing in the market. You should go through this report to ensure that you are making the right choice. The data collection results should show you that you could make enough profits when you invest in it. A small company will always aim to sell a large volume of stocks, and if you are impressed with the company and its numbers, you can invest in the stocks of that company. Remember that a company only publishes the results quarterly. Therefore, you need to look at all the results before you invest in the company.

Look at the Company Name

When choosing to invest in the stock market, you should understand that its name does matter. You must see if the company is well known and is doing well in the market. You can invest in a company that does not have any significant changes. Some people steer clear of such companies. If you are not a fundamentalist and are willing to take on a few risks, you can use technical analysis to help you make the decision. It is always good to learn more about the company if you choose to invest in shares in that company.

Understand the Company Better

You need to look at how the stock performs in the market, but it is important to spend some time understanding the company you are investing in. You need to know if the company is working on the right products and services. Understand the industry of the company. See if they are developing new products, technology, or services. Remember that whatever the company does affects the price of the stock. The best way for you to do this is to learn more about the company through fundamental analysis. You should always read the news about the company too. It is only this way that you can assess how well the company is doing. If you have any knowledge about the company or the products, you should spend some time to see where the company is heading.

When you start looking at a company, you need to ensure that you obtain the information from the right sources. Read this information carefully to understand whether the company is doing well or not. Ensure that the sources you use to obtain this information are reliable. If you get a fax, tip, or email from a person stating that one company is better than the rest, you need to make sure that you do not rush into investing. Take some time out and read about the company. Never invest in any company simply because of some information you may have received. Always conduct thorough research before you invest in the company. This is the only way you will learn if the company is doing well or not. Never waste your time or money. So, always stick to reliable sources and use that information to invest in the correct stocks.

Don't Trust Mails

You mustn't trust any emails that come from companies that claim to have enough knowledge about the stocks of other companies. These emails will also suggest the stocks that you should invest in, but the information in those emails is untrue. Companies cannot go through their investors' portfolios and suggest which stocks they should invest in. Even if a company does choose to do this, they may give you a suggestion that will not work for you. So, it is good to avoid these stocks and only invest in those stocks that you have all the information about.

Understand the Corrections

Remember that the price of stocks will be corrected in the market, and it is important that you remain patient. The price of the stock will drop when the market is correcting the price of the stocks in the market. If you are impatient, you will make a mistake and lose a lot of money. Always look at the company and make the right decisions about your investments. If a stock is either overpriced or underpriced, it means that the corrections will be made soon. Never sell your stocks in a panic and wait for the corrections to be made. You need to follow the news regularly, so you understand how or why the correction is being made.

Hire a Broker Only If Necessary

You should never hire a broker to do the job for you unless you need one. The only reason is that a broker will charge you a fee for helping you with your investments. They will also ask you to pay a commission, which will eat into your profits. You also need to remember that you need to pay your broker a fee regardless of whether you make a profit. So, they do not have to work hard to ensure that you make a profit. There are theories that companies hire brokers to increase the price of the stock in the market. They request the brokers to motivate investors to trade in a specific stock even if they do not want to invest in that stock. You will purchase these stocks if you can be swayed easily, which will lead to huge losses. You should always look for discounts online and see if you can trade independently. Avoid depending on your broker to buy and sell your stock.

Diversify Your Risks

This has been mentioned repeatedly across the book, so you can imagine how important it is for you to do this. You must always diversify your risks depending on the type of investment you make. This holds for any instrument. When you choose to invest in stocks, try to invest in stocks from different industries and sectors. If you invest in stocks only in one sector, you will lose a lot of money if the industry were to crash. It is because of this that you need to ensure that you diversify your capital. You must invest in different instruments in the market. Yes, one industry may be doing well compared to other industries, but this does not mean that you put all your money on stocks in that industry.

Money Movement

If you notice a sudden change in the price movement and the flow of money in the company, you know that the stock value will increase. If there is a sudden increase in the capital through external sources or it pumped its profits into its business, then it means that the company wants to expand. This will mean that the stock prices will rise, and it will benefit you as an investor. You must always keep track of the news and make the right decisions.

Look at the Stock Volume

If you notice that the volume of the stock has suddenly changed in the market, it is always a good idea to invest in that stock. The sudden changes in the price and volume of the stock will happen when there is some information in the news about the stock that makes people buy or sell stocks. Ensure that you capitalize on these situations so that you can make a huge profit. According to Timothy Sykes, you should always purchase a stock if you experience a high price after one year. The price of the stock will change only when the company talks about its earnings and bonuses.

Chapter 10. Advice to Minimizing Losses and Maximizing Gains

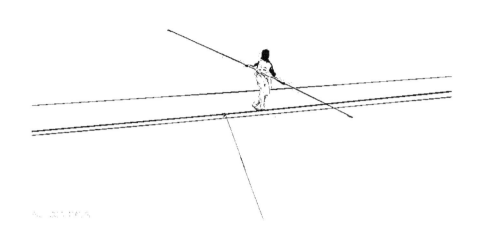

Some firms have different shares on the market. Some are good, and others are not so lucrative. How are you going to pick the right companies' stocks to make a full profit?

Well, the question is a million dollars one, but the answer is pretty easy. Before and unless you know the stock market, the answer to the million-dollar question cannot be sought. Yeah, business awareness is a must for anyone who wants to invest in stocks.

The good news is that trading on the Internet is very easy and hassle-free. All can invest in the stock at any time. Unlike other investment options on the market, there is no lock-in duration and restrictions.

However, you have to do some simple work in this sort of investment. At first, you will certainly reap the rewards of your investment if you prepare correctly and acquire ample knowledge of the workings of the stock market.

When the initial groundwork has been done, the answer to the million-dollar question can be sought. If a corporation issued public stock on the market — you bought those stocks, for instance, 100 shares at $10 each. Now, what factors will affect the price of the share? First and foremost, we must know why a specific company issues the public shares — the main purpose of shares issuance is to raise money for business expansion or pay the debt if any, and with the business increasing, the share prices often increase accordingly.

On the other hand, if you buy a share of a company and the share price falls in a few days, the company's growth curve is decreasing. Expert professionals, therefore, often recommend that investors keep an eye on major shares in the company.

Even if you have no idea what a company is, you can access information about a company, its growth curve, and its credibility in the previous industry. Many professionals recommend that they even purchase small-scale shares for full benefit.

Whenever you plan to buy a company share — gather all of the company's profile details and other important information. Following the study, purchase certain shares if you agree that a certain company share price will increase.

What Other Factors Affect the Trading Process?

Well, the website of the stock trading organization, the stockbroker, and the decision-making capacity impact the entire trading mechanism directly. It is always often easier to make a thorough market analysis on the Internet and then select the best alternative. If your fundamentals are simple, your investment will certainly give you maximum benefit. It is easier to do some simple work and then trade instead of jumping straight on the market. Now it is clear that professionals who make money on the same market have done all the required work required before the trade. So if you are a new investor and want to earn profits in a short time, first do your primary job, advise financial experts and then start trading online. Save money and build a good financial reserve to help your family better and effectively.

Options Trading — Losing Before Winning

 Many options traders were frustrated when they set options to make a profit faster. Currently, nearly 90 % of the time, your options role will lose a lot until it would ultimately gain if it's raining at all. Sounds like something you've experienced?

Yeah, this is a reality of options trading and practice that seasoned traders like me learned to embrace. Many of my positions, especially single directional ones such as a long call, actually fall into a 60% loss until they eventually return to an astounding 100% profit. Yeah, most beginners took the loss early and missed the benefit.

What is the explanation for this phenomenon?

There are three key reasons why MOST options strategies lose a lot before making a profit.

The bid/work distribution of all the options involved in one position is first and foremost. The difference between the demand price and bid price of the options contract is the bid differential. Traders purchase retail options at the requested price and sell at the sale price.

An Options Contract with a $0.90 demand price and a $0.60 offer price has a $0.30 bid transaction range. This means that if you sell the option right as you purchased it, you instantly lose $0.30. The range of requests for options is considerably large for most inventories with spreads of $0.30 and spreads of up to $0.50 in some cases.

Only in extremely liquid inventories such as the QQQQ are there spreads of $0.10. Buying out money options costing about $0.70 with a bid of $0.20 could make you lose up to 30% right when you're in a spot! This is where most beginner options traders freak out, particularly if they commit the greatest sin of options trading—put all of their money into one trading.

Secondly, none of us, either George Soros or Warren Buffett, are stock market wizards. None of us will be able to trade reliably and move the stock exactly as planned at the moment it was launched (day trading excluded because periods are very limited in day trading).

As Jim Kramer said, we should always gradually develop a role over days because we are not geniuses. Yeah, unfortunately, most of the time, the stock seems to be heading in the opposite direction the very moment you sell.

The explanation seems that most traders enter trade emotionally when the shopping is heavy, which is also the point at which the stock retreats somewhat because of the over-compensation or over-sale when purchasing put options or shortcuts.

Leveraging in options trading now works in both ways. If it makes money faster, it will lose money faster, even though the stock just marginally shifts towards your favor.

Thirdly, Feedback!

Yeah, for a certain number of contracts, most options brokers will charge a minimum of $10 per trade. For beginner traders who take very small jobs, $20 ($10 for purchases and $10 for sales) may make considerable losses, particularly when money options are purchased. Committees often greatly sacrifice nuanced techniques for alternatives with multiple legs, such as the Condor Spread.

Combine the offer for spread loss with a pullback into the market, because we're not geniuses, and you'll end up losing 60% or more the very day that you placed a stock option. Sad but true, such a drastic and rapid loss would ruin most policy losses.

That is why many traders take losses too early to see stock recovery, ultimately in the right direction. Yeah, most losses are taken before the expiry of certain options! From a recent report, 60% of all available options were shut down before expiry!

When we use options trading strategies with limited risk, we can restrict this risk to a sum that we fully expect a loss, and we can tolerate loss if the trade goes wrong. When we transact directional options, we place some small "bets" over some time, and each time, ensure that the total is small enough to lead to negligible losses if the trade goes badly.

When you traded in this way, strength and control will overpower your emotions in the face of almost an immediate 60% loss in directional options trading.

Holding control also enables non-geniuses like us to wait for the reserves where they would ideal are, as most inventories won't move the way we want them to instantly (neutral tactics for options are very different, as you would expect the inventory not to move.

If you embrace the fact that your next trade option will possibly lose money considerably before they can benefit, it means you can use only the money that you intend to lose from the beginning to have a holding power that increases your chance of winning considerably

Chapter 11. Tax Implication and How to Reduce Their Impact on Your Earnings

Ah, we come to our favorite subject, taxes! The objective in the stock market is to make money, and every time that you make money, you are going to find yourself in a position of having to pay taxes on it. Unfortunately, it's a reality we can't escape. You might delay it, but at some point, you're going to have to pay.

There are many different issues you need to be aware of when it comes to taxes. This isn't a tax advisory book, and you should consult an accountant to make sure you're doing everything right. However, we'll take a brief look at some of the main issues.

Capital Gains

Suppose that you hold an asset, and the price appreciates. If you sell it, you'll realize a capital gain — in other words, you made money. When you make money by selling appreciated assets, you owe capital gains tax. The important thing to consider is how long you held the asset.

If you held the asset for one year or less, this is a short-term capital gain. The bad news about this is short-term capital gains are considered ordinary income. That means you'll pay the regular income tax rate on your gain.

If you hold the asset for longer than a year, even if it's just a day, then it becomes a long-term capital gain.

For some reason, Congress has decided that they know that holding assets for an arbitrary period that they made up is better, and so long-term capital gains have very favorable tax rates. These are much lower than income tax rates.

The bottom line here is that you'll want to take into account how long you have held an asset (aka stocks) when selling. If you are a long-term investor and planning to hold your investments until retirement, this means that you will be paying long-term capital gains taxes on your investments when you sell them off to get the money. Of course, if your retirement is in the distant future (more than ten years away), it's hard to say what the laws are going to be.

Dividend Income

The important thing to note about dividend income when considering taxes is that it's considered to be ordinary income. There isn't anything special to consider dividend income. The one exception is dividends paid by an MLP. That's because they aren't technically dividends and you're considered a "partner" in the business. In that case, you are able to deduct depreciation from your taxes. The company passes it on to the "partners." This has huge implications. Many investors in MLPs are able to enjoy their income from the investments virtually tax-free. It's a little complicated, so if you start putting money into MLPs, you'll want to consult an accountant. The company will be sending you the appropriate forms.

Individual Retirement Accounts

One of the advantages of individual retirement accounts or IRAs is that they allow investments to grow inside of them tax-free. You can utilize this to your advantage. One way to do so is to buy dividend stocks inside the IRA and then reinvest the dividends. That way, you can continually grow your account and grow it beyond the usual limitations.

Expenses

Deducting expenses related to your investment might be problematic. The IRS isn't too friendly when it comes to deducting expenses related to investing. There is one exception, and that is if you are a day trader. Then a day trader can deduct expenses like publications they read and all the computer equipment and software services that they sign up for. But if you are doing ordinary investing, that might be a hard sell.

One way to get around it is to set up a business to run your investing. Then have the business buy all the equipment and so forth. Of course, this will inject other complications into the situation, so you'll have to weigh the pros and cons in order to determine whether or not it's really worth the extra hassle. Quite frankly, in most cases, it's not going to be.

Understanding Your Brokerage Account and Statement

You'd be surprised to know that most extremely wealthy people have taxable brokerage accounts. It provides an avenue for them to benefit from the stock market and diversify their income stream. As we've discussed earlier in this book, if you want to invest huge amounts of money and be a successful investor, you have to open a taxable brokerage account.

What is a Brokerage Account?

A brokerage account is a taxable investment account that you can use to buy and sell stocks and other securities. As the name suggests, it's opened through a brokerage firm. It's much like a bank account. You have to deposit money into your account before you can start buying and selling stocks.

You can deposit money into your account through checks or electronic funds transfers. You can also wire money to your account.

Type of Investments a Brokerage Account Can Hold

Brokerage accounts are not just for stocks. There are a number of securities that a brokerage account can hold, including:

- **Common Stock** — This represents partial ownership of a company. It usually comes with voting rights.

- **Preferred stock** — This stock usually comes with high dividend payments, but it's more expensive than common stock. Preferred stock shareholders typically don't have any voting rights.
- **Bonds** — A bond is a debt security. When you purchase a bond, the issuer (usually a government entity) owes you money. You earn money from bonds through interest rates.
- **Mutual Fund** — A mutual fund is funded by different shareholders. It's basically a pool of money that's invested in different securities. It's relatively easy to invest in a mutual fund. Plus, it's usually managed by a financial professional. You can buy different mutual funds, too, so you don't have to put all your money into one mutual fund.
- **ETF** — An ETF, or Exchange Traded Fund, is a basket of different securities that are traded like a stock. An ETF is a good investment because it has trading flexibility. It helps you diversify your investment portfolio and manage risk. It's also cheaper than a traditional mutual fund.

- **REIT** — A real estate investment trust, or REIT, is a company that either finances or operates income-producing real estate properties, such as commercial buildings. REITs usually own various income-generating real estate companies, such as hospitals, warehouses, hotels, and malls. You can invest in publicly traded REITs using your brokerage account.
- **Money Market and Certificate of Deposit** — A money market account generally represents pools of liquid mutual funds. It has higher interest rates and has a limited check-writing capacity. A certificate of deposit is basically a time deposit. For example, you agree to deposit $10,000 into your account. You can't withdraw that amount for five years, but you'll earn an interest rate throughout this period. So, if you earn $1,000 in interest per year, you're going to earn an extra $5,000 for your deposit after five years.

Cash Brokerage Accounts and Margin Brokerage Accounts

There are two main brokerage account types — cash accounts and margin accounts. A cash brokerage account requires you to deposit cash into your account. You'll have to pay for your transactions in cash and in full when you have a cash brokerage account.

A margin account, on the other hand, allows you to borrow from the broker using some of your assets as collateral to buy securities.

If you're a beginner, it's best to go for a cash brokerage account. Why? Well, margin brokerage accounts are complex and will get you buried in debt if you're not careful.

Limits of Money You Can Deposit in a Brokerage Account

As previously mentioned, other investment plans such as the IRA and 401(k) have limits, but taxable brokerage accounts do not, so you can deposit and invest as much as you want. That said, keep in mind that you do have to pay taxes for this type of investment.

How Many Brokerage Accounts Can One Have?

You can have as many brokerage accounts as you want, but keep in mind that most brokerage firms require a minimum deposit amount of $500 to $2000, so opening multiple accounts can be costly.

However, if you have unlimited resources, you can open multiple accounts with different brokerage firms.

Difference between a Discount Broker and a Full-Service Broker

There are two general types of broker:

- A full-service broker and

- A discount broker

A full-service brokerage account is great because it comes with a dedicated broker. You can call, text, or email him should you want to make an order. This broker usually knows you personally, and sometimes he knows your family. He also knows your finances intimately. He's like a financial advisor. You usually have to meet him regularly to discuss your portfolio.

Full-service brokers usually charge high commission fees. A discount broker, on the other hand, doesn't charge much. But, this type of broker usually operates online. A discount brokerage account is like a Do It Yourself (DIY) investment plan.

So, what should you choose? Well, it depends on what your priority is. If you are on a budget and you really want to save money, it's best to open a discount brokerage account. But, if you really want to have a financial adviser, it's a great idea to open a full-service brokerage account.

Understanding Your Broker's Statement

A broker's statement is a monthly report that contains the activities in your brokerage account. You can choose to receive a paper statement, but you can usually just check it online as well.

It pays to examine your statement carefully so you can spot some kind of fraud. When you first receive your income statement, you have to check to see if it looks professional. An unprofessional-looking statement is a red flag. Legitimate brokerage firms invest time and effort to make sure that their reports look polished and professional.

Here's what you'll find in your broker statement:

- **Statement Period Date** — A broker's statement reports how your investment is doing at a specific period of time, usually a month. If you don't see a statement period date, that's a red flag.

- **Account Number, Account Name, and Address** — This obviously contains your taxable brokerage account number, your name, and your present address. Be worried if this information is incorrect.

- **Contact Information** — This contains the contact information of your broker. If you don't see this anywhere in the statement, the brokerage firm you're dealing with may be dubious.

- **Name of the Clearing Firm** — This contains the name and the contact number of the clearing firm that holds your investments. FINRA rules require brokerage firms to place this information in their statements. So, be alarmed if you don't see this anywhere in your statement.

- **Account Summary** — This provides insight with regards to how your account is doing. This can help you review and assess your investment decisions.

- **Fees** — This covers the transaction and commission fees you've paid within the time period.

- **Account Activity** — This is where you can see the stocks you've bought or sold within that particular time period.

- **Margin** — If you have a margin account, you'll find this section. This contains the amount you've borrowed to purchase stocks and other securities.

- **Portfolio Detail** — This section breaks down your investment by types like stocks, bonds, or mutual funds.

Chapter 12. What to Do and What to Buy in a Down Market

Now that you have an idea of why you need to invest and some fundamental principles in investment as well as asset classes, you can invest in it. For you to start winning in a big way, you would have to put in the time. You would have to put in the effort. You would have to have the proper experience and groundwork to make that happen. And in many cases, even with the best-laid plans and with the best strategies laid out, things still don't pan out.

The better approach is to do the best with the situation you are facing. In other words, use specific strategies that would enable you to position yourself to come out ahead. They might not necessarily result in you making tons of money or experiencing truly stupendous returns, but they can position you for solid gains. The following strategies enable you to do just that.

Buy Depressed Assets

Now, this might seem straightforward. After all, this is just a reiteration of the classic investment and commercial maxim of "buy low, sell high." However, the big challenge here is in determining what constitutes a "depressed asset."

You might be thinking that a stock that was trading at $50 and pops to $150 might not be all that depressed if it fell to $100. You might be thinking, where's the depression? This is not a fire sale. It hasn't fallen enough.

If you look at the stock's trajectory and how much growth potential and market attention, it might very well turn out that the stock is headed to $300. Do you see how this works?

If that's the case, then scooping up the stock at the price of $100 after it fell from $150 is a steal. After all, buying something worth $300 for a third of its price is one heck of a bargain.

Now, the big issue here is how do you know the stock's full future value? This is where serious analysis comes in. You can't just buy stocks on hype. It would be best if you looked at facts that would inform the growth trajectory of that stock.

For example, is it a market leader? Does it have certain drugs in the approval pipeline that have little to no competition? Is it on the cusp of a breakthrough drug patent? Is it in the process of buying out its competition?

There are many factors that you should consider, which can impact the overall future value of a stock. You should pay attention to its current developments, and you should pay attention to the news cycle surrounding the company.

You should also pay attention to its industry. Is its industry fast-expanding, or is it a "sunset industry" on its last legs? If it's in a sunset industry, there might still be opportunities there because, usually, such industries witness a tremendous amount of consolidation. Whatever the case may be, always be on the lookout for the future value of a stock based on what you know now, as well as its past performance.

Dollar-Cost Averaging

What happens if you buy a stock that subsequently crashes? This happens to the very best of us. If this happened to you, don't get depressed. Don't think that you suck at investing. Don't think that all is lost. If you get caught in a downturn, it might be an amazing opportunity.

Now, it's important to note that almost all stocks experience a pullback. I have yet to come across a stock that has appreciated positively with no dips in its trading history. I'm not aware of a stock that hasn't experienced a day-to-day dip in pricing. All stocks experience a pullback. Even stocks that are well on their way to becoming breakthrough or high-valued stocks will experience dips.

What happens if you bought a stock that drops in value tremendously? Well, you have two options at this point. You can wait for the stock to keep going up and then start buying some more. You're taking bets on its recovery.

The better approach would be to use this as an opportunity. For example, if you bought, for the sake of simplicity, one share of stock at $100 a share, and the price crashes 50% to $50 a share, you can buy one share at $50, and this would average out your holdings to $75 per share.

Ideally, you should wait for the stock to drop so much and then buy a whole lot. This enables you to set your break-even point at a much lower level. For example, using the same hypothetical facts mentioned above, instead of buying one share, you buy 9 shares at $50. So, what happens is, the average price per share gets reduced to $55.

Even if the depressed stock manages to limp along and possibly pop up here and there, it doesn't have to pop up all that much to get all your money back from your position because once it hits $55, you're at break-even territory. Compare this with breaking even at $75 or, worse yet, waiting for the stock to come back to $100 a share. It's anybody's guess whether it will back to that level.

This strategy is called dollar-cost averaging, and it is very useful. You must have free cash available, and you must use that free cash at the right time.

That's how you maximize its value. That's how you fully take advantage of opportunities that present themselves. Otherwise, you might be in a situation where the stock crashes so hard that you could have broken even very easily with little money spent, but unfortunately, you were locked out because you don't have the cash to do it.

Buy Self Liquidating Assets

Another investing strategy you can take is to buy assets that pay for themselves. For example, if you spent a million dollars buying a building, but the building generates rents totaling $100,000 per year, the building pays for itself in roughly 13 years or more, factoring in taxes and other costs.

Self-liquidating assets may seem too good to be true, but they are very real. Most of this applies to certain types of real estate, like commercial properties. However, this strategy also applies to stocks and bonds.

For example, if you buy stocks that have no dividend and you buy bonds, you can use the bond interest to start paying off your stock's portfolio. Of course, this can take quite a bit of time if you factor in interest rates as well as taxes.

Smart Money Valuation

Another winning strategy is to buy into private corporations as a sophisticated investor at a much lower valuation. Now keep in mind that many mobile app companies are popping up all over the United States. You don't necessarily have to live in Silicon Valley of California to have access to these types of companies.

The great thing about these companies is that in the beginning, they require very little capital. Many require "Angel," "per-Angel," or even raw seed capital. The founder would have a rough idea of software, an app, or a website. This is the most basic stage of a company's evolution.

Now, when you come in as a source of seed capital, you can lock into a large chunk of the company's stock for a very low valuation. For example, somebody comes up with a startup idea, and the initial cost is a maximum of $1 million. If you were to invest $250,000, you have a 25% stake in the company.

You may be thinking that 25% of a company that's not worth that much, which is very, very risky, doesn't seem like a winning proposition. Well, keep in mind that after the seed stage, the company's valuation usually goes up. So, once your money has been used to push the company further along its developmental path, the company's valuation starts to go up, especially if they now have something more concrete to show other investors.

You may be asking yourself, okay, the smart money valuation thing sounds awesome. This is great in theory, but is it real? How can the Average Joe investor get in on such deals?

There are websites like Angel List and others, as well as LinkedIn groups that publicize startup projects that are actively recruiting investors. Of course, you need to do your homework and pay attention to the track record of the founders.

Chapter 13. How to Use Both Macroeconomic and Microeconomic Analysis

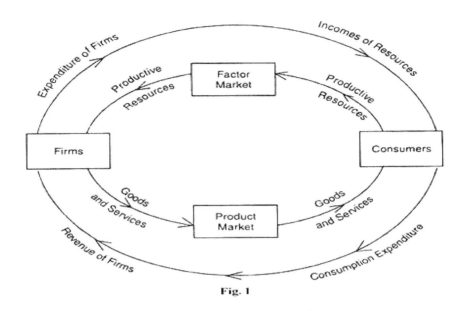

Fig. 1

You can't go to war without a weapon. You can't just buy a stock; you must do extensive research. You must learn to be your own stock analyst. This will help you make wise and sound investment decisions.

To do comprehensive stock research, you must apply two methods used in economics—microeconomics analysis and macroeconomic analysis.

Macro-Economic Analysis

As discussed earlier in this book, economic forces (such as the law of supply and demand) affect stock prices. So, before you invest in a stock, you have to use a top-down global research approach. You must look at the global trends. You must look at the big picture.

As of this writing, Airbnb is not a public company yet, but for the purpose of discussion, let's assume that it is. A lot of cities in Europe and in the United States have banned Airbnb, but it continues to grow in various cities in the world. In fact, you can find a lot of great Airbnb deals in Bali, Malaysia, Singapore, Zurich, Mykonos, and Faro. Plus, it still has a number of untapped markets. If you look at the big picture, you'll see that Airbnb is still a great investment because of its huge growth potential.

Aside from looking at the company's global overview, you must also consider other factors, such as:

Interest Rates

When the interest rate is high, it would be more costly for companies and individuals to pay their debts. This decreases their disposable income and their spending. This also affects business revenues and can drive down the stock prices.

But, when a country has a low-interest rate, people have more disposable income. They'll end up buying more stuff. This could lead to an increase in stock prices.

However, you have to take note that rising interest rates can benefit specific industries, such as the financial sector — banks, mortgage companies, lending companies, and insurance companies.

The Cyclical Nature of an Industry

Before you buy a company's stock, you have to determine if that company belongs to a cyclical industry.

Cyclical sectors such as the automobile industry and the construction industry are sensitive to the ups and downs of the economy. When the economy is good, their prices go up, but they go down when there's a recession.

Try to avoid investing in companies in cyclical sectors (unless you're very good at timing your investments). You'd want to invest in a stock that can withstand economic setbacks.

Stock Market Index

As previously discussed, an index tracks the performance of market leaders. So, in essence, it reflects the overall health of the stock market. If an index is trending up, it means that stock market players are a bit optimistic and a bull market may be happening.

Industry-Wide Research

Let's say that you want to invest in luxury brands such as Louis Vuitton (LVMH) or YSL. Before you do that, you must look into the overall health of that industry.

If you look closely, you might discover that luxury brands are not doing as well as they used to be because of online shops and China-made products.

Micro- Economic Analysis

When you do macro-economic analysis, you are looking at the economy and the industry, but understand that microeconomic analysis uses a "bottom-up" approach. This means that you have to do extensive company research.

You have to look into the different aspects of the company, such as:

- **The Company's Product** — Is the product good? Does it have loyal customers? Is the product going to be relevant ten years from now? Let's say that a music store is selling its stocks. Would you buy it? Well, let's face it: no one buys CDs anymore. We just download music from the internet or check YouTube. Technology is changing by the minute. A widely used product may become irrelevant and unnecessary in the next few years. Just look at what happened to diskettes.

- **Sales and Revenue** — Are the company earning money? Are their products doing well in the market?
- **Debt to Equity Ratio** — Is the company's debt bigger than its equity? If so, then you should run as fast as you can.
- **P/E Ratio** — If the company has a high P/E ratio, it means that it has high growth potential. However, it also means that the stock is overvalued. A low P/E ratio means that the company has low growth potential, but it also means that it's overvalued. If you're into growth investing, choose a company with a high P/E ratio. But you have to choose a company with a low P/E ratio if you're into value investing.
- **Earnings per Share (EPS)** — A company with high EPS is really doing well. It's profitable. So, assuming other factors check out (e.g. it's not using a lot of

unsustainable debt to generate the earnings), it's a good idea to invest in a company with a high EPS.

- **Company Management** — Do you trust the people managing the company? Do they engage in unethical business practices? If you don't trust the people running the company, then avoid it at all costs.

Also, make sure that the company's profit has been trending upward at least in the last five years.

Chapter 14. How to Create a Secure Financial Future

In today's scenario, where the economy hides and seeks some sort of position, financial security is a must for every individual. Although it is a broad category, financial security, however, means investment and income in the future. Look at the market, and you'll find different options for investment. Often it's hard to pick the right option.

Trading is yet another investment opportunity that offers no limits, unlike other investment strategies, but just good returns. However, as we all know, the stock market is a constantly changing environment, and we need technical analysis to learn from it; that will ensure your market success.

Unfortunately, many of us are not going to analyze it and continue to invest. The result is obvious, and that is why people often do not respond disproportionately to stock trading.

On the other hand, many of us profit from the same market, but attitudes and strategies differ. Why is one person a successful trader and another failing trader? If you know the difference in this small line, your investment strategy is guaranteed to succeed. Before you start trading, there are many things to consider:

- **Financial Strength** — Firstly, your financial strength — how much you want to invest — must be analyzed. You can start with small funds if you are a new trader. You can add more funds to your investment plan once you make money.
- **Experts in Finance** — investment is not a simple task. Proper planning is, therefore, a must. If you know market trends and trading experience, you can plan without assistance. However, if you are new and would like some assistance, please consult financial experts — they are available online and offer the best investment plan.
- **Comprehensive Market Knowledge** — A successful trader needs good market knowledge.
- **Online Stock Broke** — Because we are unable to trade directly, your broker makes all forms of trading and charges a small fee in return. It's like a connection between the trader and the stock market. You should therefore have a good broker who can

also give you advice and let you know about the most profitable company shares.

- **Technical Analysis** — A complete competitive market analysis is a must. You have to analyze stock price trends in the last 3 to 5 days, and you can predict market mood further. This research, however, does not always succeed; it still gives us an idea of the market.

- **Positive Attitude** — it is not your attitude; it is your business attitude. Those who often see the market as a risky forum affect many of us and create a negative business attitude. In that very case, you can make the wrong decision, even if you are on the right track. Therefore, you must be optimistic and try to believe in yourself.

One of the main factors for successful trading is the ability to understand the market and to adapt to changing circumstances. Once you get to know the market moods, you can better reap the advantages. Invest now and build a strong future financial reserve.

How to Choose the Right Stocks to Invest In

Mia worked in a software development company for fifteen years. She's good at her job, but she was always stressed and tired. So, she decided to give stock market investment a try in order to build a passive income portfolio that would help her retire early. She met with an old friend named Kate, a financial analyst. Kate helped her invest in high-quality and fast-growing stocks.

 After two years, Mia had earned $650,000 capital appreciation profit. She quit her job and traveled around the world. She soon used part of her earnings to establish her own graphic design company. Her $650,000 grew to over $2 million.

 Mia is living her dream life. She owns her time. She has a successful business, and she even bought a beach house in Miami.

Chloe was Mia's former colleague. Like Mia, she's been working in the software development industry for about fifteen years. She was also tired. After she heard about Mia's success, she decided to invest in stocks, too.

Chloe didn't know anything about the stock market and didn't know how to choose the right stocks. She invested in companies that were buried in debt and engaged in unethical business practices. So, she ended up losing $10,000.

A lot of people get rich through stock market investment, but many people lose huge amounts of money too. This is the reason why you should be careful in choosing the right stocks to invest in. You have to be clear about your investment goals and use the right strategies that work for you and match your risk tolerance level. You must also do extensive research before you place your bet on a stock.

Setting an Investment Objective

Before you start investing, you should be clear about what your investment objectives are. You should also decide what type of investor you want to be. Do you want to be a long-term investor? Or, do you want to be a day trader, trading stocks by the minute?

You must be clear about what you want to achieve through stock market investing. How much are you willing to invest?

How much do you want to earn each year? What are you willing to risk?

You need to set financial goals like how much you want to earn in one year or in five years. You should also set non-financial goals. Why? Well, your investment earnings are just mere tools that you can use to support your non-financial goals. So, what do you want to achieve? Do you want to have a grand wedding? Do you want to travel to a foreign country at least twice a year?

Factors to Consider in Choosing a Stock

The key to building a profitable investment portfolio is choosing the right stocks. When you're starting, buying individual stocks is costlier than investing in low-cost mutual funds. Below are the factors that you should consider in choosing stocks to invest in.

- **Growth in Earnings**

    Before you invest in a company, you should check its earnings and make sure that it's consistently growing over time. The growth doesn't have to be huge. You just have to look for an upward trend in earnings.

For example, let's say that you have an extra $3,000 and you want to invest it in stock. You're looking to invest in two companies. Company A is one of the biggest steel manufacturers in the country, while Company B produces the nation's best-selling batteries.

Take time to examine the data below:

- **Company A: Leading Steel Manufacturer**

Year	Earnings
2005	$2,158,111,202

2006	$2,160,369,000
2007	$2,080,250,000
2008	$1,988,910,000
2009	$1,888,630,121
2010	$1,780,980,011
2011	$1,761,918,870
2012	$1,709,919,450
2013	$1,670,980,689

Year	Earnings
2014	$1,659,658,905
2015	$1,640,050,814
2016	$1,590,010,110
2017	$1,550,000,289
2018	$1,499,110,980

- Company B: Leading Battery Manufacturer

Year	Earnings

2005	$750,000,905
2006	$805,963,960
2007	$815,750,690
2008	$909,530,066
2009	$915,784,210
2010	$918,974,560
2011	$990,741,632

2012	$1,101,890,390
2013	$1,156,120,450
2014	$1,190,110,000
2015	$1,220,000,980
2016	$1,240,780,360
2017	$1,310,000.550
2018	$1,399,222,080

If you look closely, you'll see that Company A has a lot more earnings than Company B. However, its revenue has been declining since 2008. This means that the company is facing problems. It could be mismanagement or a decreasing market share due to an aggressive competitor entering the space.

Company B, on the other hand, has had steady growing earnings since 2006. This company is doing something right and is more worthy of your hard-earned money.

- **Stability**

Sir Tim Berners-Lee published a paper about a proposed information management program called the "internet" in 1989. He then implemented the first successful communication between a Hypertext Transfer Protocol (HTTP) and a server a few months later.

In 1990, Berners-Lee began writing the World Wide Web (www) — the first-ever web browser. The next year, he launched the first-ever web page. This forever changed the world. This is what stock market players call a black swan.

According to risk analyst Nassim Nicholas Taleb, a black swan is an event that's hard to predict that can forever change the world. And if you're wise enough to predict or at least spot a black swan at its early stage, you're going to win big in the stock market and in business. This explains why early internet entrepreneurs like Jack Ma and Jeff Bezos are extremely wealthy.

And soon, promising internet companies decided to go public and the investors went crazy placing their eggs in the "internet business basket."

But after the tech industry got a little too crowded and the world experienced a stock market crash in 2008, the revenues of internet companies became volatile. So, a lot of investors ended up losing huge amounts of money.

Even so, this is just an example. It doesn't mean that you shouldn't invest in the tech industry. All companies are bound to lose their stock value at some point, especially during periods of recession and economic crisis.

To achieve long-term success in the stock market, you have to invest in companies that are strong and stable enough to endure unfavorable economic conditions. Erratic stock price fluctuation is not a good sign.

To illustrate this point, look at the graph below:

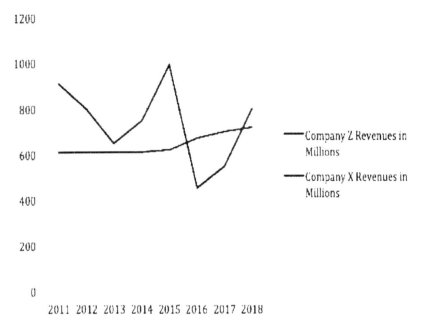

Notice that Company Z's revenue doesn't fluctuate as much as Company X's. This means that it's more stable and a good choice for long-term investment.

Chapter 15. Stock Market Strategies for Profitable Investing

Learning how to use successful bond market strategies will vary between the loss and possible profits of all your hard-earned money. These tips help you find the right investment strategies to use and avoid those that harm you more.

The Business Know

It is necessary to know the market before you can begin investment so that you can better understand how to use effective stock market strategies. Study the market as best as you can, including those stocks that are of interest to you — there are plenty of websites and other reference material that can help you get an understanding of the market.

Besides, partnering with a reputable financial advisor or creditable financial information provider is a perfect stock market strategy to understand better the market and what it can do for you.

Evite Fraud

Beginners are particularly vulnerable to fraud and schemes designed to draw prospective investors to divide their hard-playing cash. Many who fall for these sly stock market schemes won't do anything; in fact, only the scammers themselves profit from these scams!

The bottom line — most definitely if it sounds too good to be true. Equipped with the right investment strategies and expertise, you won't fall into these enticing schemes.

A Stock Broker Notice

An investment plan is a perfect way to use a stockbroker as a reliable broker will help you to decide on your portfolio and help you pick the right stock for your situation. A trustworthy broker can use his expertise to help you gain greater market knowledge, including trends, stock growth, and whether to buy or sell.

Furthermore, a stockbroker can show you even better investment strategies than you can buy. A reliable broker will happily assist you with your investments and will do everything possible to lead you in the right direction.

Learning how to play the stock market can be terrifying for beginning investors in particular. By learning about the market, avoiding schemes that are too good for you to be true, and finding a reputable stockbroker, you will learn successful stock market strategies to make your investment profitable.

It is crucial for beginners to have a solid understanding of the market and how to be as effective as possible before even beginning to invest in the stock market. The following bonds will lead you in the right direction.

Train Yourself

The first step towards being a good investor is to educate you. Take a few lessons in accounting, read as many books on investment as possible, and look online for different facets of the business and how it works for you.

Another suggestion that helps you become a better investor is to talk to a licensed stockbroker or financial advisor. A renowned advisor can provide you with direct personal information which you are not able to find in books or posts, and can also sit one-on-one with you and answer all your questions.

Take Stock Exchange Tools

Another smart tip is to use apps for some tasks. It is advisable to invest in personal finance software that can help you handle your money and track income and losses. A program that helps you monitor your stock market portfolio and trace when to buy or sell will be another software to consider; evaluate potential profits vs. risks of a specific stock, and track stock prices.

Continue to Train

One of the best investment tips, particularly for beginners, is to continue to practice until you have a good understanding of the market and its concepts. If you do not follow some other bond suggestion, it should certainly be a priority, regardless of what.

Many stock simulation programs, without taking risks and investing, will make you experience the real thing. Some of these systems are more practical than others, but all of them help you understand the idea of stock purchasing and trading.

This quick, productive tip lets you learn how to play the market and how to make it work for you. There are many stock trading tips, particularly for beginners, but you can only hope to make the most out of investing through knowledge and experience. The tips listed here are designed to help beginners learn about the market and make the best choices to succeed.

Chapter 16. COVID-19 Effects on Working with Stocks

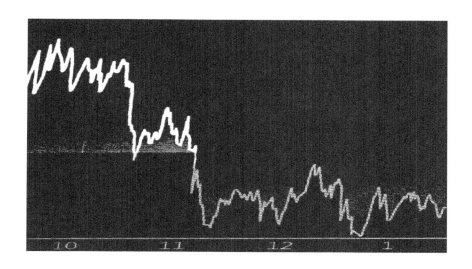

The stock market's reaction to the COVID-19 pandemic and the subsequent economic fallout has raised both fears and questions. This column delves into unexpected developments. There is evidence that shareholders favored the less distressed companies, and that credit facilities and government guarantees, lower policy interest rates, and stock price lockdowns helped to minimize the stock price decline. Fundamentals, on the other hand, only account for a limited portion of stock market fluctuations at the country level. Overall, it's difficult to argue that the correlations between stock prices and fundamentals have been shaky at best.

The World Health Organization (WHO) declared on June 8, 2020, that the COVID-19 pandemic was worsening around the world and cautioned against complacency: "the majority of people worldwide are still vulnerable to infection. "...With more than six months left in the pandemic, now is not the time for any nation to ease up on the gas." The US stock market started its fourth consecutive week of gains on the same day. The S&amp P 500 index has returned to where it was at the start of 2020, erasing the historical decline (one-third of its value) that occurred between February 20 and March 23, 2020, as if nothing had happened. As seen in the graph, this is absolutely unparalleled.

Is there something unusual about the stock market behavior during COVID-19? The reaction of financial markets poses serious concerns as the world suffers from the worst economic crisis since the Great Depression (Baldwin and Weder di Mauro 2020a, 2020b, Bénassy-Quéré and Weder di Mauro 2020, Coibon et al. 2020). Stock prices have been wildly fluctuating since the start of the crisis. They dismissed the pandemic at first, then panicked as it spread to Europe. They are now acting as if the millions of people who have been poisoned, the 400,000 deaths, and the containment of half the world's population has had no economic effects.

Paul Krugman (2020) said out loud what many people were thinking in one of his famous New York Times columns: "Whenever you consider the economic ramifications of stock prices, you want to remember three rules." To begin with, the stock market is not the same as the economy. Second, the stock market isn't the same thing as the economy. Third, the stock market is not a replacement for the economy (...). The correlation between stock performance and real economic growth, which is largely driven by the oscillation between greed and fear, has always been shaky at best. "Malkiel and Shiller (2020)," two other well-known economists, have also discussed the stock market's strange conduct in the face of the pandemic. The suspected stock market irrationality, according to Malkiel, is just "apparent," and the COVID-19 crisis does not "imply that markets are dysfunctional" since there are no arbitrage possibilities and stock markets remain difficult to beat. "Speculative prices can statistically mimic a random walk, but they are not as bound to genuine knowledge (...), says Shiller. The infectious stories about the coronavirus had their own internal complexities that were only tangentially linked to the truth."

What lessons can be learned about stock market actions from the COVID-19 crisis? This debate is particularly important for financial economists, but it is also important because the general public has a negative perception of stock markets, which should worry us (Rajan 2015) — especially after the COVID-19 crisis placed science and 'experts' to the test (Aksoy et al. 2020), without sparing economists.

A rapidly growing body of research looking at stock market reactions to the COVID-19 pandemic is already providing some insights. Although the stock market's actions during the pandemic could seem spontaneous, irrational, or even insane at first glance, closer observation shows that they did not respond randomly. Several studies have shown that stock markets are effective at discounting the most vulnerable companies: those that are financially fragile, vulnerable to international value chain disruption, vulnerable to corporate social responsibility, or less resilient to social distancing (Alburque et al. 2020, Ding et al. 2020, Fahlenbrach et al. 2020, Pagano et al. 2020, Ramelli and Wagner 2020). Furthermore, it appears that, at least in the medium term, stock market declines are linked to analyst forecast revisions (Landier and Thesmar 2020). We approach these papers from a macroeconomic standpoint. While the studies described above provide useful details, some questions remain unanswered.

What has been the response of the stock market to the COVID-19 pandemic? How do we understand the disparities in responses around countries? Are there any macroeconomic or institutional factors that influence stock market response across countries, and if so, which ones? Are these disparities the product of how governments treated the pandemic? How have financial markets responded to nationwide lockdowns and economic policies aimed at 'flattening' the curves of infection and recession? (2020 Gourinchas)

We discuss how stock markets have incorporated public knowledge about the COVID-19 pandemic and subsequent lockdowns in our recent paper (Capelle-Blancard and Desroziers 2020). Despite the fact that the COVID-19 shock was global, not all countries were affected in the same way, and they did not react in the same way. This high heterogeneity is something we take advantage of. We want to understand the differences in stock market responses by looking at the situation in each country prior to the crisis, as well as the subsequent containment measures (social distancing and stay-at-home orders) and economic policies (fiscal and monetary) that were introduced during the crisis.

From January to April 2020, we consider a panel of 74 nations, which can be divided into four phases: incubation, outbreak, fear, and rebound. We gathered regular data on stock index prices, COVID-19 total cases and deaths, global market sentiment and volatility, government responses to the outbreak, and various indicators of mobility for each region (or lack thereof).

Three main results emerge about stock market reactions during the COVID-19 pandemic. First, after initially ignoring the pandemic (until February 21, 2020), financial markets responded strongly to the rise in the number of infected people in each country (February 23 to March 20, 2020), with volatility increasing as fears about the pandemic increased. Following central bank intervention (23 March to 20 April 2020), however, news of the health crisis no longer seemed to bother shareholders, and shares rebounded all over the world. Second, it appears that country-specific characteristics had little, if any, impact on stock market responses. Stock markets in countries more vulnerable to the pandemic did not respond as strongly, either because of systemic economic fragility (for example, indebted countries) or because of exposure to transmission vectors (for example, countries with 'at-risk' populations). Third, the number of COVID-19 cases in neighboring (but mostly wealthy) countries piqued investors' interest. Fourth, the fall in stock prices was mitigated by credit facilities and government guarantees, lower policy interest rates, and lockout measures.

Finally, do capital markets take into account all available information? In fact, we can see the glass as either half-full or half-empty. On the one hand, the stock market's behavior during the COVID-19 pandemic is not entirely coincidental. Our research indicates that the reaction of stock markets was affected by health policies introduced during the crisis to restrict virus transmission and macroeconomic policies aimed at supporting businesses, rather than the situation of countries prior to the crisis. Fundamentals, on the other hand, only account for a (very) small portion of stock market volatility. It's difficult to deny that the connection between stock prices and fundamentals has been anything but loose, as Krugman and Shiller have claimed.

Conclusion

There are also many different types of investments, orders, and such that the individual may make. It is crucial that the investor knows the differences between these and can decide on which methods the investor wishes to invest in. However, the investor must know the pros and cons of each to reach that conclusion. The investor must educate himself or herself before making any further decisions on their investments and strategies for trading. There are many elements of the stock market that one must familiarize themselves with; the more that you know, the better the chance of you receiving a high return on your investment is.

Stock market investing can be very powerful for any person looking to create wealth or build a side income. Among all the asset classes, stock investments have generated the best returns historically. Consequently, it is beneficial for you over the long term that you develop a sound understanding of this highly profitable investment avenue.

The next step is to follow this through and begin your quest as a stock investor. It is important to begin by setting goals for yourself as an investor. You must consider all of the variables involved in investing. Setting goals will help provide you with a sense of direction. By using this as a reference, you may decide on which path of investing you will choose. What will be the time period of your investment? Will you purchase individual stocks or ETFs? How much risk are you willing to take in your investments? These questions, among others, must be answered to provide you with clear goals in your investing. After this, you may create an account, fund your account, and start trading. There must be research done, and you must select your stocks. After this, you are on the path to success in trading.

After you have accomplished this, you must continue to conduct research on the market, monitor your stocks, and manage your portfolio. Being an investor is an ongoing process. This can really help you to get started in learning about stock, and it may serve as a reference guide throughout your stock investing career. There will constantly be changes in the economy, the stock market will fluctuate every day, and the stocks themselves will continuously move. However, the basic concepts of stock will always be helpful to know, and this provides its readers with those basics that are necessary for one to be successful in stock investing.

The goal is to help investors, especially those who are just getting started with investing in the stock market, to learn the basic concepts of the stock market that will help them to initiate the trading process and become both successful and profitable in their investments.

Stock investing requires discipline, patience, and thoughtful analysis. Diversification is an essential strategy for successful stock investing. Keeping your emotions in check is also a crucial part of becoming a successful investor. A long-term approach to stock investments provides many times good returns.

By reading it to the end, you are proving that you are disciplined and ready to work hard! Many rookie investors spend their money investing blindly. Unlike the majority, you have taken your time to acquire knowledge to make wise decisions. Good job!

OPTIONS TRADING

A Crash Course Guide to Making Money for Beginners and Experts:

How to Invest in the Market through Profit Strategies to Buy and Sell Options

Anthony Sinclair

Introduction

An option is a financial contract called a derivative contract. It allows the owner of the contract to have the right to buy or sell the securities based on a specified period's agreed-upon price.

As the name suggests, there is no obligation in this type of transaction. The trader pays for the right or the option to buy or sell a transaction such as security, stock, index, or ETF (exchange-traded fund). An option is a contract.

The option derives its value based on the value of the underlying asset hence the term derivative contract. This contract states that the buyer agrees to purchase a specified asset within a certain amount of time at a previously agreed-upon price. Derivative contracts are often used for commodities like gold, oil, and currencies, often in US dollars. Another type of derivative is based on the value of stocks and bonds. They can also be based on interest rates such as the yield on a specified amount of time Treasury note as a 10-year Treasury note.

In a derivative contract, the seller does not have to own the specified asset. All he must do is have enough money to cover the price of the asset to fulfill the contract. The seller also has the option of giving the buyer another derivative contract to offset the asset's value. These choices are often practiced because they are easier than providing the asset itself.

Securities come in several types. The great thing about securities is that they allow a person to own a specified asset without taking its tenure. This makes them readily tradable because they are good indicators of the underlying value of the asset.

The trader can exercise the option at the strike price up until the expiry date reaches. In Europe, a trader can only exercise the right to the option at the strike price exactly on the expiry date. We will more largely focus on the American way of trading options, which allows for exercising right on or before the expiration date.

Trading options and trading stocks are different because stocks and options have different characteristics. Stocks share ownership in individual companies or options, and this allows the stock trader to bet in any direction that he or she feels the stock price is headed.

Stocks are a great investment if you are thinking of long-term yields, such as for retirement and have the capital. They are very simplistic in the approach in that the trader buys the stock and wagers on the price that he or she thinks will rise at a certain time in the future. The hope is that the price will increase in value, thus gaining the trader a substantial yield.

The risk of investing in stocks is that stocks can plummet to zero at any moment. This means that the investor can lose his or her entire investment at the drop of a hat because stocks are very volatile from day to day. They react to world events such as wars, politics, scandals, epidemics, and natural disasters.

On the other hand, options are a great option for traders who would like flexibility with timing and risks. The trader is under no obligation and can see how the trade plays out over the time specified by the option contract. In that period, the price is locked, which is also a great appeal.

Trading options also require a lower investment compared to stocks typically.

Another great appeal for options reading is that the specified period is typically shorter than investing in stocks. This allows for regular buying and selling as options have different expiration dates.

The drawback that makes some people hesitate in trading options is that it is more complex than trading stocks. The trader needs to learn new jargon and vocabulary such as strike prices, calls and puts to determine how he or she can set up effective options. Not only does the trader have to learn new terms, but he also must develop new skillsets and the right mindset for options trading.

There are several advantages to trading options, and they include:

The initial investment is lower than with trading stocks. This means that the options trader can benefit from playing in the same financial market as a stock trader without paying as much upfront. This is called hedging.

The options trader is not required to own the asset to benefit from its value. This means that the trader does not incur the cost associated with the asset. Costs can include transportation and storage fees if applicable.

There is no obligation to follow the transaction. Whether the trader exercising a call or put option, at the end of the day, the loss is limited because the trader is only obligated to pay for the contract and nothing more. Only if the trader feels it worth it does he or she take action to move forward with exercising the contract.

The options trader has many choices. Trading options give the trader great flexibility.

The strike price freezes the price. This allows the options trader the ability to buy or sell the asset on or before the expiration date without the worry of fluctuating prices.

Options can protect an asset from depreciating market prices. This is a long-term strategy that can protect assets from drops in market prices. Exercising a call allows the trader to buy the asset at a lower price.

The trader can earn passive income from assets that he or she already owns. You can sell call options on your assets to earn income through traders paying you premiums.

Successful options traders weigh the pros and cons carefully and implement strategies to minimize the costs and potential losses while leveraging ways to make maximum profit.

BEGINNERS

Chapter 1. What Are Options Trading and the Best Market

An option is an agreement that lets in (but doesn't require) a monetary expert to purchase or sell a hidden instrument like a security, ETF, or even list at a foreordained cost over a specific timeframe. Buying and selling options are achieved on the alternatives advertise, which exchanges agreements dependent on protections. Purchasing a choice that allows you to shop for shares sometime in the future is called a "name alternatives." However, shopping for an option that permits you to promote shares sometime within the no longer too distant future is referred to as a "put alternatives."

Nonetheless, alternatives are not a similar thing as shares considering they don't communicate to proprietorship in an organization. What's more, even though fates use contracts truly as options do, options are viewed as a lower risk because of the way that you may pull back (or leave) An option contract anytime. The price of the alternatives (its top rate) is, therefore, a degree of the hidden useful resource or security.

There are various types of alternatives — call and put options — which offer the speculator the right (however not commitment) to promote or purchase protections.

Call Options

A call option is a settlement that offers the monetary expert the privilege to purchase a particular measure of offers (regularly 100 for each transaction) of specific protection or object at a predefined fee over a selected take look at of time. For instance, name options might enable a supplier to purchase a selected movement of quantities of either stock, bonds, or even unique gadgets like ETFs or lists at a later time (via the termination of the agreement).

In case you're purchasing a name option, it implies you need the stock (or other security) to head up in price with the aim that you can make an advantage off of your settlement through training your entitlement to purchase those shares (and commonly quickly offer them to capitalize on the benefit).

The rate you are paying to buy the name alternatives is referred to as the top-notch (it's the expense of purchasing the agreement which will permit you to, in the long run, buy the stock or security). In this sense, the top rate of the name alternative is just like an in advance installment like you'll put on a house or vehicle. When buying a name, alternatively, you concur with the dealer on a strike fee. You are given the option to purchase the security at a foreordained price (which doesn't change till the agreement terminates).

Be that because it may, for what motive would a monetary expert use option? Purchasing alternatives are essentially wagering on stocks to go up, down, or to help an exchanging position in the marketplace.

The cost at which you consent to buy the fundamental protection utilizing the opportunity is called the "strike cost," and the cost you pay for purchasing that alternatives settlement is referred to as the "superior." When identifying the strike fee, you're wagering that the gain (in general, a stock) will go up or down in fee. The quantity you're deciding to buy that wagered is top-notch, which is a stage of the estimation of that benefit.

There are various types of options — name and put alternatives — which offer the financial expert the right (yet now not commitment) to sell or purchase protections.

Thus, call alternatives are additionally a lot of identical protection — you are paying for a settlement that terminates at a set time but allows you to buy protection (like a stock) at a foreordained cost (which won't move up regardless of whether or not the fee of the stock available does). In any case, you have to reestablish your options (typically week after week, month to month, or quarterly premise). Thus, alternatives are constantly encountering what's referred to as time rot — which means their well worth decompositions after a few times.

For name alternatives, the decrease in the strike fee, the extra inherent well worth the name alternative has.

Put Options

On the opposite hand, a put opportunity is an agreement that gives the speculator the privilege to sell a particular measure of offers (once greater, often one hundred for every transaction) of specific safety or ware at a predefined value over a specific time fashionable. Much the same as name options, a put option permits the broking the right (however no longer commitment) to sell security via the agreement's termination date.

Much the same as name alternatives, the fee at which you consent to sell the stock is known as the strike fee, and the top class is the fee you are purchasing the put opportunity.

Put options paintings likewise to calls, besides you need the safety to drop in fee in case you are purchasing taken care of alternative to make again (or sell the put alternatives and while you parent the fee will pass up).

On the despite name options, with put alternatives, the better the strike price, the greater the intrinsic well worth the put alternatives have.

Long As Opposed to Short Options

Not in any respect like distinctive protections like fates contracts, are alternatives changing usually a "long" — which means you're buying the alternatives with the expectancies of the cost going up (in which case you will buy call alternatives)? In any case, irrespective of whether you purchase put options (appropriate to sell the safety), you are as but shopping extended options.

Shorting an option is promoting that alternative. However, the blessings of the deal are restricted to the premium of the opportunities — and the hazard is boundless.

Chapter 2. How Much Capital Do You Need to Trade

There are too many risks in this type of trading. Capital is a basic requirement to start any business. Does options trading require too much capital? No. When starting on options trading, it is better to start with small capital to avoid massive trading risks.

Many are the individuals who utilize much of their cash for trading during their first days, which is so dangerous. Such individuals end up having too many risks to handle, and finally, they make up their minds to close their businesses. I do not want you to fall into such a mess. Do your thing with the right speed.

Start options trading with a reasonable small amount. Do not brag off that you got everything under control. You will lose even the only cash you had. Starting with less money has a high likelihood of fewer risks in trading. I bet you can now handle a few risks and be able to continue with your trading.

How to Start Options Trading

Now with the basic knowledge of options trading, I will provide you with a few details on how to start an options trading journey.

- You should look for an options trading broker. The key to successful options trading is your broker. There exist legit and non-legit brokers in options trading. Some of the tips for selecting a good broker include the following:

- Do some research on the broker first. You need to be keen and alert before opening a brokerage options trading platform. Different brokers will approach you with different platforms. Do not rush or assume everything is good; do some research on the best brokers. Make sure you spend your cash well by paying for a good options trading platform. It will help you a lot because your trading performance depends on your platform. Choose a broker with good ratings.

- Charges lower commissions. Some brokers tend to exploit traders by charging high commissions to beginners. You should weigh different commission offers of different brokers before settling on one. Some even charge no commission to traders. You should prefer brokers with fewer commissions. Payment of high commissions periodically can mess you up with losses, and you may find it even hard to secure your trading capital. Do not accept to pay high commissions. You also need to make some savings other than wasting money while paying commissions.

- A simple user interface platform. There is a wide variety of software with different functionalities and features. Some software has a simple user interface, while others are too complex for you to use. You should choose a platform with a simple and clear user interface that enables you to make your trades with less struggle. Some platforms can waste your precious time when you struggle too much searching on the Internet on how you operate them. Make your work easier by handling software that is according to your level.

- Trading tools for research. You should also consider factors like tools that are present on the platform. Do not purchase a platform with no tools. It will be hard for you. Platform tools ease your trading and make your performance excellent. The tools here may include charting tools, research tools, and even tools that alert you on any market changes that may arise.

- Do some testing on the brokerage platform. Do not be that kind of a careless trader who does things for the sake of doing with no precautions. You need to be cautious enough since this is an income-generating activity. You should test on a brokerage software before making up your mind about purchasing it. Check on the reliability and stability of the software and be 100% sure that this is the platform you will use for your trading. Ensure the software is not that type of platform that crashes down unexpectedly. You might miss crucial trade while fixing your software.

- Be approved to trade options. You need to be approved by the broker in charge before purchasing and offering options for sale. They normally have their ways of approving you, like checking your experience and the money that you have. It aids in avoiding risks for the customers. You cannot escape this step.

- Get a clear understanding of the technical analysis. Options trading is a technical field. You need to have the technical analysis techniques of trading options. The technical aspects include reading charts, know about the volume of stock, and also moving averages. Trading charts mostly analyze price behavior in the market. You will handle the aspects many times while trading. Perfect your technical knowledge and be cautious with them.

- Take advantage of mock trading accounts. Using real accounts when starting options trading is a risky game. You can lose a lot of cash within a short time duration. Mock accounts exist for a reason. You should test your trading skills in the mock accounts, learn a few tricks, and perfect your skills. The advantage of using a mock account is that there is no loss of money since they mostly provide virtual money. It prepares you for real trading. You should take advantage of them and learn a lot. Utilize them for a while and do some evaluations on your returns. When everything works out well, face real trading and shine.

- Utilize limit orders. It is risky to rely on market prices since price behavior change with time. You should utilize limit orders when trading. A limit order is a type of order that enables you to purchase market securities at an agreed price. Using this type of order shuns you from incurring losses in options trading.

- Revise your strategies with time. After entering into the options trading, with time, you need to revise your strategies. Utilize the working strategies more often and get rid of unsuccessful trading strategies. You should not have many strategies that do not bring good performance. Few working strategies are better than having multiple ones that do not help you.

- Register and join in options trading platforms. Joining forums comprised of other options traders is another way of how to get started in options trading. Forums are platforms for different people with different experiences and opinions. You can learn mistakes made by others in trading. It is part of growing in options trading. So why shouldn't you give it a try?

- Study and learn about trading metrics. Having your returns maximized is also another way of getting started in options trading. Traders normally use different trading metrics such as delta, gamma, theta, and Vega. You should learn and practice them for massive returns.

Chapter 3. Basic Options Strategies

Traders often jump into options trading with little understanding of options strategies. With a bit of effort, traders can learn to take advantage of flexibility and power. Strategies are usually laid in the trading plan and should strictly implement in every options trading move that is likely to be involved.

Collars

The collar strategy was established by holding several shares of the underlying stock available in the market where protective puts were bought and the call options sold. In this kind of strategy, the options trader is likely to protect the capital used in the trading activities rather than the idea of acquiring more money during trading. This kind is considered conservative and somewhat much more critical in options trading.

Credit Spreads

It is presumed that the biggest fear of most traders is a financial breakdown. In this side of strategy, the trader gets to sell one put and then buy another one.

Covered Calls

Covered calls are the right kind of strategy where a particular trader sells the right for another trader to purchase his or her stock at some strike price and get to gain a proper amount of cash. However, there is a specific time that this strategy should utilize and, in a case where the buyer fails to purchase some of the stock and the expiration date dawns, the contract becomes invalid right away.

Cash Naked Put

Cash naked put is a kind of strategy where the options trader gets to write at the money or out of the money during a particular trading activity and aligning some specific amount of money aside to purchase stock.

Long Call

It is the most basic strategy in options trading and one that is quite easy to comprehend. In the long-call strategy for options trading, aggressive option traders who happen to be bullish are pretty much involved. It implies that bullish options traders end up buying stock during the trading activities with the hope of it rising shortly. The reward is unlimited in the long-call strategy.

Short Call Option

The quick-call strategy is the reverse of the long call one. Bearish kind of traders is so aggressive in the falling out of stock prices during trading in this kind of strategy. They decide to sell the call options available. This move considers being so risky by the experienced that options traders believe that prices may drastically decide to rise once again. It significantly implies that large chunks of losses are likely to be incurred, leading to a real downfall of your trading structure and everything involved in it.

Long Put Option

First things first, you should be contented that buying a put is the opposite of buying a call. So in this kind of plan, when you become bearish, that is the moment you may purchase a put option. Put option puts the trader in a situation where he can sell his stock at a particular time before the expiration date reached. This strategy exposes the trader to a mere kind of risk in the options trading market.

Iron Condor

The iron condor involves the bull call spread strategy, and the bear put strategy all at the same time during a particular trading period. The expiration dates of the stock are still similar and are of the same underlying stock. Most traders get to use this strategy when the market is expected to experience low volatility rates and with the expectation of gaining a little amount of premium. Iron condor worked in both up and down markets and was believed to be economical during the up and down markets.

Married Put

On this end, the options trader purchases options at a particular amount of money and at the same time to buy the same number of shares of the underlying stock. This kind of strategy is also known as the protective put. It is also a bearish kind of options trading strategy.

Cash Covered Put

Here, one or more contracts sold with 100 shares multiplied with the strike price amount for every particular contract involved in the options trading. Most traders use this strategy to acquire an extra amount of premium on a specific stock they would wish to purchase.

Long Butterfly

This strategy involves three parts where one put option is purchased at particular and then selling the other two options at a price lower than the buying price and purchasing one put at an even lower price during a specific trading period.

Short Butterfly

In this strategy, three parts are still involved were a put option sold at a much higher price and two puts then purchased at a lower price than the purchase price and a put option is future on sold at a much lower strike price. In both cases, all put bear the same expiration date, and the strike prices usually are equidistant as revealed in various options trading charts. A short butterfly strategy is the opposite way of a long butterfly strategy.

Long Straddle

The long straddle is also known as the buy strangle, where a slight pull and a slight call are purchased during a particular period before the expiration date reaches. The importance of this strategy is that the trader bears a high chance of acquiring reasonable amounts of profits during his or her trading time before the expiration date is achieved.

Short Straddle

In this kind of strategy, the trader sells both the call and put options at a similar price and bearing the same expiration date. Traders practice this strategy with the hope of acquiring reasonable amounts of profits and experience various limited kinds of risks.

Reverse Iron Condor

This kind of strategy focuses on benefiting some profits when the underlying stock in the current market dares to make some sharp market trade moves in either direction.

Iron Butterfly Spread

Buying and holding four different options in the market at three different market prices is involved in the trading market for a particular trading period.

Short Bull Ratio

The short bull ratio strategy is used to benefit from the amounts of profits gained from increasing security involved in the trading market in a similar way in which we usually get to buy calls during a particular period.

Strap Straddle

Strap straddle strategy uses one put and two calls bearing a similar strike price and with an equal date of expiration and also containing the same underlying stock that is usually stagnant during a particular trading period. The trader utilizes this type of strategy for the hope of getting higher amounts of profits as compared to the regular straddle strategy over a specific period of the trading period.

Strap Strangle

This strategy is strong, where more call options are purchased as compared to the put options and a bullish inclination is then depicted in various trading charts information.

Limit Your Risk

A good reason to go with buying options is that you will be able to limit your risk down to just the amount of money that you pay for the premium. With other investment options, you could end up losing a lot of money, even money that you did not invest, to begin with, but this does not happen when you are working with options.

Let's say that you saw that the prices of cows were about to go up. You could pay some money upfront and enter into a contract with someone else to sell your five cows for $ 2000. At this point, since you are working with an options contract, you did not buy the cows upfront.

On the other hand, if you had gone up to the other person and purchased those cows straight up for a cost of $ 10,000, you could end up in trouble. For this example, the price of the cows may end up falling by $ 500, rather than going up by $ 500, and you would end up losing $ 2500 in the process. Since you went into the options contract though, you would stand to lose no more than $ 250 if the prices were to fall afterward. You still stand to lose some money, but it is a lot less than you would have lost otherwise.

You will find that when you are working with options, it can provide you with some good leveraging power. A trader will be able to buy an option position that will imitate their stock position quite a bit, but it will end up saving them a lot of money in the process.

Let's say that you saw that there was an opportunity to make a profitable trade, you were only able to spare about $ 1000 to purchase the stock, but you didn't know that options were available. If we were still talking about the cows from before, you would not be able to purchase even one cow for the money (remember that they are about $

2000 each without the options contract). So you would completely miss out on the possibility of making a profit.

But, if you decided to purchase with an options contract, rather than buying the underlying asset outright, the dynamics have completely changed. If you look into options contracts, you will be able to make more purchases and potentially more money compared to some of the other stock choices you can make.

Going back to the idea of the cows, the market price at the beginning of this trade is $ 2000. For a regular cattle trader, one who doesn't know anything about options had the $ 2000 in hand and believed that the price of the cattle is going to go up; he would only have the opportunity to purchase on a cow. If the cost of the cows goes up to $ 2500, this trader will only be able to make a profit of $ 500. It isn't bad, but since there is a significant risk with this option, it is not always the best.

On the other hand, a trader who knows a bit about options will be able to do things a bit differently. If you had $ 2000, you could choose to purchase eight options contracts, with a premium of $ 50.t This means that you now have the purchasing rights for a total of 40 cows rather than the one cow the other trader had.

With the same profit of $ 500 per cow, your profit would be $ 18,000 (this includes the $ 500 per cow minus the $ 2000 you spent in the beginning to purchase the contracts). You earned thousands of dollars more compared to the original trader, but you used the same amount of money to get started.

Chapter 4. Risks Management in Options

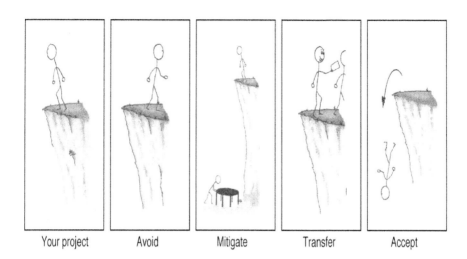

Many experienced options traders find it relatively easy to make money but holding it can prove harder. As anyone can do, there must be another dimension to the trading option that has been ignored so far; otherwise, any trader would be through. This is the risk management dimension. Most of what professional traders can do is manage Risk; play defense and try to keep profits. If a market maker manages to keep a third of the bid-ask range, it will be very successful in the long run. Danger management tension is a key differentiator between amateurs and experts. There are two things to remember when putting risk management in perspective.

At times, it's fun to "take a shot" when you make a trade. This could have been for some reason. You might want to start trading with a new strategy. You might have a hunch that you simply can't get the hard evidence to validate. And you might need to do a swap to help the trader. It is never necessary, however, to "take a shot" when handling the Risk. Risk management is far too important to take the chance. You just don't need to have any patience for errors.

Professional option trading is not about making significant, unforgettable trades. It is about making low, predictable gains and keeping risks under control.

We should take care of the risks in the order of their Risk. We will split the risks into three groups.

- **Primary Risks**
  - Inventory
  - Delta
- **Secondary Risks**
  - Gamma
  - Jump risk
  - Vega (including skew and calendar risk)
- **Tertiary Risks**
  - Correlation risk
  - Rho
  - Dividend risk
  - Buy-in risk
  - Early exercise

- Strike risk

- Pin risk

Stock Risk – Dividends and Buy-in Risk

Let's have a look at the case when a corporation declares a special dividend. Assume the stock is at $100, so we're long 1,000 out of a one-year 80 strike order. Assume the interest rate is negative, and the conditional uncertainty is 30%. The sum of this option is 23.53. When the corporation pays a dollar dividend, the interest of the call will decrease to 22.73. We're suddenly wasting $80,000. Remember that this is not going to support being hedged in the underlying. The dividend is a gain to those who hold the shares, not to those who own the options.

It doesn't happen very often. So, when it does, it can be a huge concern. In 2004, Microsoft paid a special dividend of $3.08 as the shares traded $29.97. Beware of businesses sitting on a lot of funds. It is, of course, entirely probable to be harmed if we have a long stock, and the planned dividend is that.

Nonetheless, the business option tends to be better at forecasting this. Generally, the rumors of payout cuts are beginning to surface well in advance of the real reduction, and the option sales are continuing to be sold at a lower cost. Finally, regular dividend yields appear to be much smaller than special dividends, so the cut in the normal dividend will not be as expensive as the declaration of a special dividend.

Pin Risk

Pin risk arises as the underlying interest reduces the effective interest of the option at expiration. Anyone short of these options is exposed to pin risk. The main Risk is that it is difficult to determine whether the decision will be exercised.

Note that since the Risk of a pin is triggered by the probability of a given investor having an unplanned role in the underlying stock that he eventually must liquidate, it is not a matter of cash-setting options. There we earn cash for any expiring shares. Cash does not need to be unwound or liquidated until the economy is reopened. Nevertheless, cash-setting options have their expiration wrinkle.

Forward Risk

For most options, as the in-the-money option expires, we will obtain the corresponding position at the bottom (a long position for long calls, a short position for medium calls, a short position for short calls, and a medium position for short calls). As we keep the offset position as a buffer at the start, we're not going to have a net advantage until expiry.

That is not the case for cash-setting options. Here we usually have a future or another traded commodity, but at the end of the day, we obtain cash. As a result, our expiry status does not balance our shield. If we don't want to be directional, we need to flatten our options for deltas in the month to come.

Irrelevance of the Greeks

As the expiration approaches, the utility of most Greeks as Risk controls declines. Vega and rho are now obsolete, as the trend towards zero, as the time to expiration tends towards zero. More specifically, gamma and theta become confusing.

At the time of expiration, gamma is infinite if our preference is at the money and zero otherwise. That's because we're precisely at a point where the option switches from being equal to the underlying situation to being useless. The delta will transform from one to zero when the underlying price passes the hit. To avoid incurring huge hedging costs, the investor will postpone worrying about persistent delta hedging and then wait until he is confident that the delta option has exceeded its expiring value and then hedged. This isn't as troubling as it seems, because it is expected to entail a change of less than a buck.

Theta is also becoming unreliable. Less significance of theta starts earlier than gamma, sometimes yielding very odd numbers many days before the expiry date. The main issue here is that theta has been configured to display the deterioration of option interest over one day. Normally, this is a good thing as it transforms theta into a number that is directly relevant, however close to its expiry, it becomes irrational when theta shifts too rapidly for one day.

Expiring at a Short Strike

As the expiration approaches, the utility of most Greeks as Risk controls declines. Vega and rho are now obsolete as they move towards zero, as the time to expiration tends towards zero. More specifically, the gamma and theta become confusing.

At the time of expiration, gamma is infinite if our preference is at the money and zero otherwise. That's because we're precisely at a point where the option switches from being equal to the underlying situation to being useless. The delta will transform from one to zero when the underlying price passes the hit. To avoid incurring huge hedging costs, the investor will postpone worrying about persistent delta hedging and then wait until he is confident that the delta option has exceeded its expiring value and then hedges. This isn't as troubling as it seems because it is expected to entail a change of less than a buck.

Theta is also becoming unreliable. Less significance of theta starts earlier than gamma, sometimes yielding very odd numbers many days before the expiry date. The main issue here is that theta has been configured to display the deterioration of option interest for one day. Normally, this is a good thing as it transforms theta into a number that is directly relevant, however close to its expiry, it becomes irrational when theta shifts too rapidly for one day.

Chapter 5. Volatility in the Market

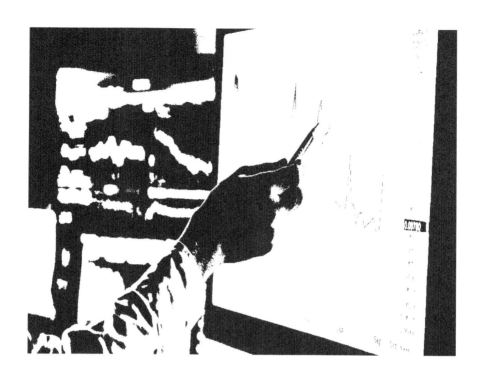

We can define volatility as a statistical measure of the levels of fluctuations of stock, shares, or the entire market. The value is calculated as the ASD or annualized standard deviation of the price swings of security in terms of daily percentage. The value is expressed as a percentage.

Historical Volatility

Historical volatility is simply a measure of a security's volatility in the past. When computing this figure, you will have to define a specific period for consideration. One of the most common figures used for historical volatility is 20 days. This specific measure approximates total trading day numbers within a month.

Implied Volatility

Another useful term is implied volatility. This measures the volatility that is implied by the prevailing market price of the stock's options. Implied volatility is computed using one of the main option pricing models, like the Black Scholes Model. Using this or similar models, you can work out volatility where a mathematical relationship has been established relating to the price of an option and the volatility of the underlying stock.

Implied volatility provides insights into the market's view of the options contracts' underlying security. It can be determined by making use of the following:

- Option's current market price
- The value of the underlying security
- Expiration dates
- The strike prices
- Any applicable interest rates
- Any applicable dividend yields

In an ideal situation, we would expect the implied volatility figure to be the same for all options that have the same expiry date. This is regardless of the strike price that was used in our computations. In practice, however, this is hardly accurate because the figures we get vary mostly due to strike prices. This variation in volatility is known as the volatility skew.

The Impact of Volatility on Options Trades

We have already established what the term volatility means in options trading. It is simply a measure of the size and rate of the price change of the underlying security. High volatility implies a high option premium. The reverse is also true.

If you can accurately assess the value of statistical volatility for the underlying security, you will be able to use this value in a pricing model for purposes of computing a fair market price for the option. It is crucial that, as an options trader, you keep in mind the fact that changes in volatility can greatly impact your trades either negatively or positively.

Historical volatility generally measures the speed at which a futures commodity or stock price has moved in the past. This enables you to predict with some degree of accuracy, its expected movement in the future.

For instance, if we have a vehicle that is traveling at 50 miles per hour, we can determine how many miles it will travel for the entire year.

Distance = speed * time

In our case, distance = 50 mph * 24 hours/day * 365 days/year = 438,000 km

If everything remains constant, then we can accurately predict the distance that the car will cover. However, in real life, this is hardly the case because the car could make stops, break down sometimes, and so on. The same is true for stocks and options. Although our calculations depend on known factors, if the variables keep changing, the outcome could be different.

How to Compute Historical Volatility

Historical volatility is quantifiable and is based largely on previous changes to a futures or stock options contract. To calculate this figure, you need to consider the past prices and all price changes, then average them out into a percentage.

For instance, you can consider the historical volatility for 10 days. If you have the price change for 10 days in percentage terms, you should subtract the daily percentage price variations to find deviations from the average daily change for the period.

One of the most common methods that can be used to compute historical volatility is the close-to-close changes in percentage for daily values. There is another method known as the high minus low prices. Another approach would be to take an average of low, high, and median prices. The purpose of all these models is to obtain some intraday information that is usually not included in a close-to-close system.

It is also advisable to spend a few moments calculating historical volatility as well as the trending vs. trading range markets. A stable trend will likely emerge, and it can go either up or down but will not affect the size of percentage price changes.

While the changes in average daily price may increase, historical volatility as calculated may become smaller. Also, it is possible to demonstrate that historical volatility figures can increase if the average daily price reduces in size regardless of the market trends. One of the most popular methods uses 10 days of daily percentage price changes. This information is then used also to compute a standard deviation. Commonly used are 20 and 30 days and specific time frames for your computations.

How to Compute Implied Volatility

It is a lot easier to look at implied volatility with common pricing models such as the Black-Scholes model. You will need to have at least five inputs or variables. These variables are:

Chapter 17.   Historical volatility (or statistical volatility)

Chapter 18.   Strike price

Chapter 19.   Stock price

Chapter 20.   Risk-free interest rate

Chapter 21.   Number of days to expiration

With these inputs, you will receive a more accurate and reliable theoretical option price. However, most of the time, the markets do not set the fair value price for the same option. Options prices will normally deviate from these theoretical values. The fair price is a result of the input of five independent variables.

In general, if the market price exceeds the theoretical price of an option, then market participants such as traders and investors have added a premium to the price. A lot of these concepts are best viewed with real-life examples.

Commodity options usually portray excellent volatility. When the markets portray high volatility, then traders should be careful of buying options straight up. It would be a lot better to sell than to buy at this point. When the volatility is low, then options buyers should start buying.

Chapter 6. Typical Beginners Mistakes in Options

"Well, now we know what not to do."

Inexperienced traders are often warned away from purchasing options that are out of the money as being a greater risk than the ultimate reward is likely to be. While it is true that a short expiration time coupled with an out of the money option will frequently look appealing, especially to those with a smaller amount of trading capital to work with, the issue is that all of these types of options are likely to look equally appealing which leaves them with no way to tell the good from the bad.

As a more experienced trader, however, you have many more tools at your disposal than the average novice which means that, while risky, cheap options have the potential to generate substantial returns, as long as you keep the following in mind while trading them.

Ignoring the Statistics Behind Options Trading

One of the biggest mistakes that most newbie options traders make is that they forget the probability is a real thing. When you check a potential stock before purchasing an option, it's important to understand that the history of an option is important when deciding whether or not you should be investing in it, but so are the odds and probability surrounding whether or not a particular event is going to occur.

For example, a common strategy that investors use is to leverage their money by investing in cheap options so that this will help to prevent big losses on a stock that they actually own shares of. Of course, this is a good strategy, but nothing works one-hundred percent of the time. Make sure that if the rules of probability and simple ratios are telling you to stay away from a deal, you listen to the facts staring you in the face. Wishful thinking will come to bite you later on.

Being overzealous: Frequently, when new options traders finally get their initial plan just right, they become overzealous and start committing to larger trades than they can realistically afford to recover from if things go poorly. It is important to take it slow when it comes to building your rate of return and never bet more than you can afford to lose.

Regardless of how promising a specific trade might seem, there is no risk/reward level at which it is worth considering a loss that will take you out of the game completely for an extended period of time. Trade reasonably and trade regularly and you will see greater results in the long-term guaranteed.

Not Being Adaptable

The successful options trades know when to follow their plans but they also know that no plan will be the right choice, even if early indicators say otherwise. There is a difference between making a point of sticking to a plan and following it blindly and knowing which is one of the more important indicators of the separation between options trading success and abject failure. This means it is important to be aware of when and where experimentation and new ideas are appropriate and when it is best to toe the line and gather more data in order to make a well-reasoned decision.

This also means having several different plans in your options trading toolbox and not just resolutely sticking to the first one that brings you a modicum of success. This is crucial as there are certain plans that will only work in specific situations and knowing which to use when, in real-time, will lead to significantly greater returns on a more reliable basis every single time.

Likewise, an adaptive options trader knows that market conditions can change unexpectedly and is prepared to respond accordingly. This means understanding when the time is right to go in a new direction, regardless of the potential risks that doing so might entail.

Sometimes a good trader has to make a leap of faith, and a trader who is successful in the long term knows what signs to look for that indicate this type of scenario is occurring in real-time. Unfortunately, this type of foresight cannot be taught and instead must be found with experience.

As long as you keep the appropriate mindset regarding individual trades, any new strategy that is attempted will result in valuable data, if nothing else. It is important to understand that learning not to use a specific course of action a second time is always valuable, no matter the costs. Working to build this into your core trading mindset will lead you to greater success in a wider variety of situations in the long term.

Ignoring the Probability

Always remember that the historical data will not apply to the current trends in the market at all times which means you will always want to consider the probability as well as the odds that the market is going to behave the way it typically does. The odds are how likely the market is to behave as expected and the probability is the ratio of the likelihood of a given outcome. Understanding the probability of certain outcomes can make it easy to purchase the proper options to minimize losses related to holdings of specific underlying stocks.

When purchasing cheap options, it is important to remember that they are always going to be cheap for a reason as the price is determined by the strike price of the underlying stock as well as the amount of time remaining for the option to regain its value, choose wisely otherwise you are doing little more than gambling and there are certainly better ways to gamble than via options trading.

Not Considering Exotic Options

An exotic option is one that has a basic structure that differs from either European or American options when it comes to the how and when of how the payout will be provided or how the option relates to the underlying asset in question.

Additionally, the number of potential underlying assets is going to be much more varied and can include things like what the weather is like or how much rainfall a given area has experienced. Due to the customization options and the complexity of exotic options, they are only traded over the counter.

While they are undoubtedly more complex to get involved with, exotic options also offer up several additional advantages when compared to common options, including:

- They are a better choice for those with very specific needs when it comes to risk management.

- They offer up a variety of unique risk dimensions when it comes to both management and trading.

- They offer a far larger range of potential investments that can more easily meet a diverse number of portfolio needs.

- They are often cheaper than traditional options.

They also have additional drawbacks, the biggest of which is that they cannot often be priced correctly using standard pricing formulas. This may work as a profit instead of a drawback, however, depending on if the mispricing falls in favor of the trader or the writer.

It is also important to keep in mind that the amount of risk that is taken on with exotic options is always going to be greater than with other options due to the limited liquidity each type of exotic option is going to have available.

While some types are going to have markets that are fairly active, others are only going to have limited interest. Some are even what are known as dual-party transactions which means they have no underlying liquidity and are only traded when two amiable traders can be found.

Not Keeping Earnings and Dividend Dates in Mind

It is important to keep an eye on any underlying assets that you are currently working with as those who are currently holding calls have the potential to be assigned early dividends, with greater dividends having an increased chance of this occurrence.

As owning an option doesn't mean owning the underlying asset, if this happens to you, then you won't be able to collect on your hard-earned money. The early assignment is largely a random occurrence which means if you don't keep your ear to the ground, it can be easy to get caught unaware and be unable to exercise the option before you miss the boat.

Along similar lines, you are going to also always want to be aware of when the earnings season is going to take place for any of your underlying assets as it is likely going to increase the price of all of the contracts related to the underlying asset in question.

Additionally, you will need to be caught up on current events as even the threat of influential news can be enough to cause a significant spike in volatility and premiums as well. In order to minimize the additional costs associated with trading during these periods, you are going to want to utilize a spread. Doing so will minimize the effect inflation has on your bottom line.

Chapter 7. Important Trading Principles to Follow

You need to take it a step further by applying principles that will reinforce that plan. Think of that trading plan as the foundation of your house of success. The policies below are the bricks to develop your home into what you want it to be.

Ensure Good Money Management

Money is the tool that keeps the engine of the financial industry performing in good working order. You must learn to manage your money in a way that works for you instead of against you as an options day trader. It is an intricate part of maintaining your risk and increasing your profit.

Money management is the process whereby monies are allocated for spending, budgeting, saving, investing, and other procedures. Money management is a term that any person with a career in the financial industry, and particularly in the options trading industry, is intimately familiar with because this allocation of funds is the difference between a winning options trader and a struggling options trader.

Below you will find tips for managing your money so that you have maximum control of your options day trading career.

Money Management Tips for Options Traders

- Define money goals for the short term and the long term so that you can envision what you would like to save, invest, etc. Ensure that these are recorded and easily accessed. Your trading plan will help you define your money goals.
- Develop an accounting system. There is a wide range of software that can help with this, but it does not matter which one you use if you can establish records and efficiently track the flow of your money.
- Use position sizing to manage your money. Position sizing is the process of determining how much money will allocate to entering an options position. To do this effectively, allocate a smart percentage of your investment fund toward individual options. For example, it would be unwise to use 50% of your investment fund on one option. That is 50% of your capital that can potentially go down the drain if you make a loss in that position. A good percentage is

using no more than 10% of your investment fund toward individual option positions. This percentage allocation will help you get through tough periods, which eventually happen without having all your funds lost.
- Never, ever invest money that you cannot afford to lose. Do not let emotion override this principle and cloud your judgment.
- Spread your risks by diversifying your portfolio. You expand your portfolio by spreading your wealth by investing in different areas, add to your investments regularly, being aware of commissions always, and knowing when to close a position.
- Develop the day trading styles and strategies that earn you a steady rate of return. Even if you use scalping where the returns are comparatively small, that constant flow of profit can add up big over time.

Ensure That Risks and Rewards Are Balanced

To ensure that losses are kept to a minimum and that returns are as high as they can be, options day traders should use the risk/reward ratio to determine each and to make adjustments as necessary. The risk/reward ratio is an assessment used to show profit potential concerning potential losses. It requires knowing the potential risks and profits associated with an options trade. Potential risks manage by using a stop-loss order. A stop-loss order is a command that allows you to exit a position in an options trade once a certain price threshold has reached.

Profit targeted using an established plan. Potential profit calculates by finding the difference between the entry price and the target profit. It is calculated by dividing the expected return on the options investment by the standard deviation.

Another way to manage risks and rewards is by diversifying your portfolio. Always spread your money across different assets, financial sectors, and geographies. Ensure that these different facets of your portfolio are not closely related to each other so that if one goes down, they don't all fall. Be smart about protecting and building your wealth.

Develop a Consistent Monthly Options Trading System

The aim of doing options trading is to have an overall winning options trading month. That will not happen if you trade options here and there. You cannot expect to see a huge profit at the end of the month if you only performed 2 or 3 transactions.

You need to have a high options trading frequency to up the chances of coming out winning every month. The only way to do that is to develop a system where you perform options trades at least five days a week.

Consider a Brokerage Firm That is Right for Your Level of Options Expertise

There are four essential factors that you need to consider when choosing a broker, and they are:

- The requirements for opening a cash and margin account.
- The unique services and features that the broker offers.

- The commission fees and other fees charged by the broker.
- The reputation and level of options expertise of the broker.

Look at these individual components to see how you can use them to power up your options day trading experience.

Every options trader needs to open a cash account and margin account to be able to perform transactions. They are simply tools of the trade. A cash account is one that allows an options day trader to perform operations via being loaded with cash. Margin account facilitates transactions by allowing that to borrow money against the value of security in his or their account. Both types of accounts require that a minimum amount deposited. It can be as few as a few thousand dollars to tens of thousands of dollars depending on the broker of choice. You need to be aware of the requirements when deliberating which brokerage firm is right for you.

Broker Services and Features

There are different types of services and features available from various brokerage firms. For example, if an options trader would like to have an individual broker assigned to him or her to handle his or her account personally, then he or she will have to look for a full-service broker. In this instance, there minimum account requirements that need to meet. Also, commission fees and other fees are generally higher with these types of brokerage firms. While the prices are higher, this might be better for a beginner trader to have that full service dedicated to their needs and the learning curve.

On the other hand, if an options trader does not have the capital needed to meet the minimum requirements of a full-service broker or would prefer to be more in charge of his or her option trades, then there is the choice of going with a discount brokerage firm. The advantage to discount brokerage firms is that they tend to have lower commissions and fees. Most internet brokerage firms are discount brokers.

Other features that you need to consider when choosing a brokerage firm include:

- Whether or not the broker streams real-time quotes.
- The speed of execution for claims.
- The availability of bank wire services.
- The availability of monthly statements.
- How confirmations achieve, whether written or electronic.

Commissions and Other Fees

Commission fees paid when an options trader enters and exits positions. Every brokerage firm has its commission fees set up. These typically developed around the level of account activity and account size of the options trader.

These are not the only fees that an option trader needs to consider when considering brokerage firms. Many brokerage firms charge penalty fees for withdrawing funds and not maintaining minimum account balances — the existence of costs such as these cuts on options trader's profit margin. Payment of fees needs to be kept to a minimum to gain maximum income, and as such, an options trader needs to be aware of all charges that exist and how they are applied when operating with a brokerage firm. It needs to be done before signing up.

Broker Reputation and Options Expertise

You do not want to be scammed out of your money because you chose the wrong brokerage firm. Therefore, you must choose a broker that has an established and long-standing reputation for trading options. You also want to deal with a brokerage firm that has excellent customer service, that can aid in laying the groundwork for negotiating reduced commissions and allows for flexibility.

Ensure That Exits are automated

Even though I have stated that emotions should set aside when trading options, we are all human, and emotions are bound to come into the equation at some point. Knowing this is imperative that systems develop to minimize the impact of emotions. Having your exits automated is one such step that you can take to ensure that emotions are left out when dealing with options day trading. Using bracket orders facilitates this.

A bracket order is an instruction given when an options trader enters a new position that specifies a target or exit and a stop-loss order that aligns with that. This order ensures that a system is set up to record two points — the goal for-profit and the maximum loss point that will tolerate before the stop-loss comes into effect. The execution of either order cancels the other.

CRASH COURSE

Chapter 8. Buy an Equity at a Lower Price

$$\frac{30 \text{ Owned Shares}}{100 \text{ Total Shares}} = 30\% \text{ Equity Stake}$$

$$\frac{30 \text{ Owned Shares}}{150 \text{ Total Shares}} = 20\% \text{ Equity Stake}$$

Low margins can be very useful when trading. To use them successfully, they must be integrated into the overall pattern. The basic idea is to enter the market as soon as it breaks out of the state of equilibrium that exists. If the price rises sharply from this point on and then falls back down there, an increase in demand is expected. This is a classic double bottom. In combination with the Accumulation / Distribution, this becomes the basis for an interesting trading approach. Choose only the trades in the direction of the thrust. Place stops at the opposite end of the short bar.

Trading Beams with Large Margins

A wide-span bar can be either bullish or bearish, depending on where it appears in the formation. If it appears at the end of a buy peak, then it is to be classified as bearish, at the break from a formation, however positive. Most beams with a large span are followed directly by a correction beam. The buy zone is in the lower half of the bar, and the profit-taking area is located at around 50% to 100% of the span above the high of the bar. Of course, this only applies to short-term traders. The course tends to be varied, with a short track following a long bar. Of course, this is not always the case, and the definition of a wide-span bar is subjective. This is where the art of chart reading comes into play. This ability can only be learned by analyzing many charts over the years.

Purchase Zones

The buy zone describes the lower half of a push. While the relapses are causing the price to rise, the buying zone also moves upwards. In these areas, you should look for opportunities to get started. Before you open your position, you should know where to set the stop and set a price target. Mark the buy zone, the stop loss, and the area of the price target in the chart. Do not chase after a quick course! Among the countless stocks, there is always a good candidate for a better start. Opt for a boarding area. The following steps could help:

- Buy only in the purchase zones.

- Place your stop loss immediately after opening your position.

- Be sure to close the position when you reach the winning zone. Is this done by means of a stop, or are you simply selling? Any possibility is a compromise: if you sell, the price could rise even higher. Waiting for the stop to be triggered will often result in significant portions of the potential win.

The following options are available:

- Make the stop tighter.

- Close only half the position. So, your decision is only half wrong or half correct.

- Close your position at the first sign that the supply outweighs the demand.

- Use a shorter time frame to set the stop. For example, if you trade on a daily chart, choose a 30-minute chart to place your stop more accurately.

The Stop

If you do not know what you are risking, you risk everything. There is no stop-loss option that is equally satisfactory for everyone. Everyone has to find out for himself which ratio of risk to the potential profit he feels comfortable with. Here are some suggestions for placing stop orders:

- Three ticks below the low of the last or penultimate fulcrum

- An average range below the closing price or the low of the day on which the purchase was made

- 50% of the breakout or break-in after opening the day after entering the position. This stop works especially well when combined with the other possible stops. For example, a value sometimes opens below a stop at a level, which then turns out to be the low of the day. We like to see it move about eight ticks or half the span of the previous bar after opening.

- Three ticks below the lower low or lower end of the last two bars

- Close the position after three bars, if it is not yet in the profit zone.

- Release the trade and try to exit without loss if the trade runs too far against you after the opening and your stop is not triggered. Do not think about a possible profit anymore. Their only interest is the stopping and preservation of your capital.

It is of utmost importance to always have a good plan ready for your investment. When opening a position, ask yourself if this is a long-term investment for five or ten years or not. Then you should not panic in the face of short-term price fluctuations. Are you a trader? Unfortunately, many people set their exit point or stop loss according to the following criteria:

- The stop-loss is at a point where the losses are already huge.

- The stop is based on the general market situation. If the whole market collapses, my positions will be closed.

- As soon as everyone is frantically trying to close their positions in my stock quickly, then I sell too.

Profit Taking

If you have a long position and the price goes into profit, then you can protect your profit by:

- Best selling

- Sell when a closing price is below an opening.

- Sell when the price falls after the opening by half the average range.

- Set the stop below the previous day's low.

- Sell when the price closes below the two previous closing prices and below the opening.

- Sell at the third strong positive bar of the next smaller time frame. For example, if the price breaks into the profit zone on the weekly chart, then you sell after the third consecutive day in a row.

Anticipation

The following factors are important in anticipating the completion of a pattern or reversal. You can build parts of a position at an early stage before all criteria are met. Remember: The stated goal is to make profitable trading and not to be in the market at 90% of all price moves. Learn to settle for small pieces of the market. Either you secure your profits by means of a best-order, or you sell at the first sign that the supply exceeds the demand.

- The seven possible times to anticipate a pattern are:
- The closing price of the bar, if a short spread indicates a low supply or low demand.
- An opening course in the direction of completing the pattern.
- An outbreak after opening in the direction of completing the pattern.
- An outbreak after 30 minutes towards the completion of the pattern.
- The course is midway through the opening and in the direction of completing the pattern.
- At the closing price if the pattern is fully developed.
- For a correction movement after completing the pattern.

For many patterns, it can be seen that the price will fall back into the buy zone, but the pattern will be completed above the buy zone. Then it has to be decided on a case-by-case basis which measure is the right one.

The Time-Break-Out Rule

A common approach is to trade the breakout from the first 30-minute bar, with the stop loss at the other end of this bar. This approach has been tested using S & P's market data over 14 years. Trading according to this rule leads to huge losses. It should be noted that this method has been profitable in recent years. But one must always keep in mind the fact that how dangerous it can be, if too short a test period is chosen to check a method. When entering a position, the 30-minute rule may be useful, but as with most tools, isolated use will not work.

Price Gaps

Normally, a positive price gap is considered a sign of strength and a buy signal. In verifying this assumption, it turned out that the exact opposite is true. The review was based on two methods:

- Sale with a positive price gap.

- Sale on a positive price gap, but only if the price falls back to the previous day high.

For purchases, the opposite applies. Both approaches were tested by computer without stops and as day trades. The second approach turned out to be almost twice as successful as the first. It is used approximately 60 times a year per future. The course must go in your direction before doing anything. This signal provides a clear market advantage, but in most cases does not make up for the fees and slippage.

But when combined with other filters and more meaningful stop management, this is a valuable addition to your trading arsenal. Coincidentally, the review found that this could be a profitable trading system for bonds.

This pattern is very similar to a pattern developed by Larry Williams called Oops. The starting point is the same, but we do not know which entry and exit criteria were used by him. The information can be reused as follows:

- The signal is likely to be more reliable if the price has already gone one way and the expected end of that price movement is within range. Then this could be a good way to realize profits and perhaps build up counter positions.

- Other ideas are:

- Watch out for introductory signals on reverse movements of the last closing price, several previous closing prices, and several previous highs and lows.

- Consider setting a half-span stop after boarding.

- Watch price gaps above or below a cluster of close closing prices.

- Look for a reversal after half the gap in the price gap before opening a position.

These simple computer tests will tell you quickly whether such an opening with a price gap will give you a technical advantage in view of past price developments or not. Larry Williams and Toby Crabel have made a name for themselves in this field. Whole volumes could be filled solely with the study of price movements in relation to the opening and the movement away from the opening price.

Chapter 9. Options Pricing

Stock:	AMZN		Price	38.70		Expires:	1 month
	Call Option					Put Option	
Intrinsic Value	Time Value	Option Price	Strike Price	Intrinsic Value	Time Value	Option Price
3.70	0.30	4.00	35.00	0.00	0.17	0.17
0.00	0.65	0.65	40.00	1.30	0.55	1.85
0.00	0.05	0.05	45.00	6.30	-0.20	6.10
		= In the Money				

Stock:	AMZN		Price	38.70		Expires:	9 months
	Call Option					Put Option	
Intrinsic Value	Time Value	Option Price	Strike Price	Intrinsic Value	Time Value	Option Price
3.70	6.41	10.11	35.00	0.00	4.00	4
0.00	7.50	7.50	40.00	1.30	4.80	6.10
0.00	4.97	4.97	45.00	6.30	3.00	9.30
		= In the Money				

Options traders need to comprehend extra factors that influence an option's price and the complexity of picking the right technique. When a stockbroker becomes acceptable at foreseeing the future price movement, the person may believe it is a simple change from options, but this isn't accurate. Options traders must deal with 3 shifting parameters that influence the price: the underlying time, volatility, and security. Changes in any of these factors affect the option's value.

Option pricing hypothesis utilizes factors (exercise price, stock price, interest rate, time to expiration, volatility) to value an option hypothetically. It estimates an option's reasonable value, which traders join into their techniques to maximize profits. Some ordinarily utilized models to value options are Black-Scholes, Monte-Carlo, and Binomial Option Pricing. These speculations have wide margins for error because of deriving their values from different assets, typically the cost of an organization's basic stock. There are scientific formulas intended to compute the fair, reasonable value of an option. The broker inputs known factors and finds a solution that depicts what the option should be worth.

The essential objective of any option pricing model is to compute the probability that an option will be worked out or be in-the-money (ITM) at lapse. Basic asset value (stock value), interest rate, exercise price, time to expiration, and volatility, which is the number of days between the computation date and the option's exercise date, are usually utilized variables that are input into logical models to derive an option's hypothetical fair value.

Here are the general impacts that factors have on an option's cost:

Strike Price and Underlying Price

The value of puts and cuts are influenced by changes in the fundamental stock cost in a generally clear manner. When the stock cost goes up, calls should gain value since you can purchase the underlying asset at a lower cost than where the market is, and puts should diminish. In like manner, put options should increase in value, and calls should drop as the stock value falls, as the put holder gives the right to sell stock at costs over the falling market cost.

That pre-determined price to purchase or sell is known as the option's exercise price or strike price. Suppose the strike price permits you to purchase or sell the basic at a level that allows for a quick profits purchase, discarding that exchange in the open market. In that case, the option is in-the-money (for instance, a call to purchase shares at $10 when the market cost is currently $15, you can make a prompt $5 profit).

Like most other monetary resources, options costs are affected by prevailing interest rates and are affected by interest rate changes. Put option and call option premiums are affected contrarily as interest rates change lose value while calls benefit from rising rates. The inverse is genuine when interest rates fall.

The impact of volatility on an option's price is the most difficult concept for beginners to comprehend. It depends on a measure called statistical (also known as historical) volatility, SV for short, looking at past value developments of the stock over a given timeframe.

Option pricing models necessitate the trader to go in future volatility throughout the life of the option. Normally, options traders don't generally know what it will be and need to guess by working the pricing model "in reverse." The merchant knows the cost at which the option is trading and can inspect different factors, including dividends, interest rates, and time left with a bit of research. Subsequently, the main missing number will be future volatility, which can be evaluated from different information sources.

Factors That Affect an Option's Price

You cannot price an option until you realize what makes up its worth. An options trade can turn into a mind-boggling machine of legs, numerous orders, Greeks, and adjustments. However, if you don't have the foggiest idea about the essentials, what are you attempting to achieve?

When you take a look at an option chain, have you considered how they generated every one of those prices for the options? However, these options are not created randomly but rather calculated out utilizing a model, for example, the Black-Scholes Model. We will dive further into the Black-Scholes Model's seven components and how and why they are utilized to determine an option's cost/price.

Like all models, the Black-Scholes Model has a shortcoming and is a long way from perfect.

History of the Black-Scholes Model

The Black-Scholes Model was distributed in 1973 as The Pricing of Options and Corporate Liabilities in the Journal of Political Economy. It was created by Myron Scholes and Fisher Black as an approach to evaluate the price of an option after some time. Robert Merton later distributed a subsequent paper, further extending the comprehension of the model. As with any model, a few assumptions must be comprehended.

- The rate of profit for the riskless asset is constant.

- The more the option will be worth, the underlying follows, which expresses that move in an unpredictable and random path.

- There is no riskless profit, arbitrage, opportunity.

- It is possible to lend and borrow any amount of money at a riskless rate.

- It is possible to purchase or short any amount of stock.

- There are no charges or costs.

The model has seven factors: strike price, stock price, interest rates, types of option, dividends, time of expiration, and future volatility.

Stock Price

If a call option permits you to purchase a stock at a pre-determined cost later on, then the higher that cost goes, the more the option will be worth.

Which option would have a higher worth:

- A call option permits you to purchase TOP (The Option Prophet) for $100 while it is trading at $80 or

- A call option will enable you to buy TOP for $100 while it is trading at $120

Nobody will pay $100 for something they can purchase on the open market for $80, so our option in Choice 1 will have a low worth.

All the more alluring is Choice 2, an option to purchase TOP for $100 when its worth is $120. In this circumstance, our option worth will be higher.

Strike Price

The strike price follows the same lines as the stock price. At the point when we group strikes, we do it as in-the-money, at-the-money, or out-of-the-money. When a call option is in-the-money, it implies the stock price/cost is higher than the strike cost. The stock price is not exactly the strike price when a call is out-of-the-money.

A TOP call has a strike of fifty while TOP is presently trading at $60. This option is in-the-money.

The stock price is not exactly the strike price when a put option is in the money. A put option is out-of-the-money when the stock price is greater than the strike price.

A TOP put has a strike of twenty while TOP is presently trading at $40. This option is out-of-the-money.

In-the-money options have a greater value contrasted with out-of-the-money options.

Type of Option

This is likely the easiest factor to comprehend. An option is either a call or a put, and the option's estimation will change appropriately.

- A call option gives the holder the option or right to purchase the basic at a predefined cost within a particular timeframe.

- A put option gives the holder the option or right to sell the hidden at a predefined price within a particular timeframe.

If you are long a call or short a put, your option value increments as the market moves higher. Suppose you are short a call or long a put your option value increments as the market goes lower.

Time to expiration

Options have a constrained life expectancy; thus, their worth is influenced by the progression of time. As the time to expiration upturns, the value of the option increments. As the time to termination draws nearer, the value of the option starts to diminish. The value starts to quickly diminish within the last 30 days of an option's life. The additional time an option has till termination/expiration, the option needs to move around.

Interest Rates

The interest rate has a nominal effect on an option's value. When interest rates rise, a call option's value will rise, and a put option's value will decrease.

To drive this idea home, how about we take a look at the dynamic procedure of investing in TOP while trading at $50.

- We can purchase 100 shares of the stock altogether, which would cost us $5,000.

- Instead of purchasing the stock altogether, we can get long an at-the-money call for $5.00. Our all-out expense here would be $500. Our underlying cost of money would be littler, and this would leave us $4,500 leftover. Also, we will have a similar prize potential for half the risk. Presently we can take that additional money and invest it somewhere else, for example, Treasury Bills. This would create a guaranteed return on our investment in TOP.

The higher the interest rate, the more appealing the subsequent option becomes. In this manner, when interest rates go up, calls are a superior investment, so their cost likewise increments.

On the other side of that coin, if we look at a long put versus a long call, we can see an impediment. We have two options when we want to play an underlying drawback.

- You can short a hundred shares of the stock that would produce money into the business and earn interest in that money.

- You long a put which will cost you less money by and large but not put additional money into your business that produces interest income.

The higher the interest rate, the more appealing the primary option becomes. Accordingly, when interest rates rise, the value of put options decreases.

Dividends

Options don't get dividends, so their value varies when profits are discharged. When an organization discharges dividends, they have an ex-dividend date. If you own the stock on that date, you will be granted the dividend. Additionally, on this date, the estimation of the stock will diminish by the number of dividends. As dividends increment, a put option's value likewise increments, and a calls' value declines.

Volatility

Volatility is the main evaluated factor in this model. The volatility that is utilized is forward. Forward volatility is the proportion of implied volatility over a period later on.

Implied volatility shows the "simplified" development in a stock's future volatility. It discloses to you how traders think the stock will move. Implied volatility is constantly communicated as a percentage, non-directional, and on a yearly premise.

Chapter 10. Tips and Tricks in Stocks

This is a much better and more successful strategy. Here are some helpful tips and tricks that should guide you as you trade online in options.

The Price of Any Stock Can Move in 3 Basic Directions

These directions are up, down, and no movement at all. Depending on the kind of call that you have, you can leverage this movement to make a profit or at least avoid incurring losses.

Plenty of first-time traders and investors assume that prices of securities will go either up or down. However, this is the wrong school of thought because sometimes there is no movement at all in the price of stocks and shares. This is a very important fact in the world of options trading.

There are plenty of real-life, practical examples that show a particular stock or share which did not move significantly for quite a lengthy period. For instance, the KOL share traded within a $4 range for a total of 23 days. If you had invested money in either a call option or a put option through this stock, you would have lost money.

A purchase of a call option is usually with the hope that prices will go up. In the event that prices do rise, then you will make a profit. At other times, the prices will remain the same or even fall. In such events, if you have an out-of-the-money call, the option will most likely expire, and you will lose your investment. In the event that the price remains stagnant and you have an in-the-money option, then you will at least recoup some of the money you invested.

There will be sometimes when frustrations engulf you. This is when you just sit and watch prices start to skyrocket just a couple of weeks after the options you purchased had expired. This is often an indicator that your strategy was not on point and you did not give it sufficient time. Even seasoned traders sometimes buy call options that eventually expire in a given month and then the stock prices rise sharply in the following month.

It is therefore advisable to purchase a longer-term call option rather than one that expires after a single month. Now, since stocks move in 3 general directions, it is assumed that close to 70% of options, traders with long call and put options suffer losses. On the other hand, this implies that 70% of options sellers make money. This is one of the main reasons why conservative options traders prefer to write or sell options.

Before Buying a Call or Put Option, Look at the Underlying Stock's Chart

Basically, you want to find out as much information as possible about the performance and worth of an underlying stock before investing in it.

You should, therefore, ensure that you take a serious look at the chart of the stock. This chart should indicate the performance of the stock in the last couple of days. The best is to look at a stock's performance in the last 30 and 90 days. You should also take a look at its last year's performance.

When you look at the charts, look at the movement of the shares and try and note any trends. Also, try and observe any general movement of the shares. To identify the trend of a particular stock, try and draw a straight line along in the middle of the share prices. Then draw a line both above and below so as to indicate a channel of the general flow of the share.

Chart Readings and Buying Call Options

Let us assume that you wish to invest in a call option. Then you should ask yourself if the stock price is likely to rise and why. If you think that the stock will rise and trade at a higher level, then you may be mistaken, unless something drastic happens or new information becomes evident. New information can be a shareholders' meeting, impending earnings announcement, a new CEO, product launch, and so on.

If there is a chart showing the presence of support at lower prices and stock prices fall to that level, then it may be advisable to buy call options. The call option will be a great bet when prices are down because prices will very likely head back up. However, never allow greed to occupy your mind. When you see a profit, take and do not wait too long.

Chart Readings and Buying Put Options

Now, supposing the stock chart indicates a solid resistance at a higher price. If the stock is beginning to approach this higher level, then it is possible that the price might begin to move in that direction as well. So as the price moves, expect to gain small but significant profits. Avoid greed, so anytime the stock price falls, simply move in and make some money.

Chart Readings for Purchase of Call and Put Options

Now, if your chart readings indicate that the shares are within the lower levels of their range, then it is likely that daily changes in price will send it towards the middle of the range. If this is so, then you should move in and make a profit as soon as the price tends upwards. Even minor profits such as buying at $1 and selling at $1.15 mean a 15% profit margin.

Find Out the Breakeven Point Before Buying Your Options

Now, you need to identify a call option that you wish to invest in, especially after studying its performance on the market. Before buying, however, you should work out the breakeven point. In order to find this breakeven point, you will have to consider things such as the commissions charged and the bid spread.

It is very important that you are positive that the underlying stock of your options will move sufficiently so as to surpass the breakeven point and earn a tidy profit. You should, therefore, learn how to work out the breakeven point in an options trade.

Calculating the Breakeven Point

As an options trader, you need to know how to calculate and find the breakeven point. In options trading, there are basically 2 break-even points. With short-term options, you need to make use of the commission rates and bid spread to work out the breakeven point. This is if you intend to hold on to the options until their expiration date.

Now, if you are seeking short-term trade without holding on to the options, then find out the difference between the asking price and bid price. This difference is also known as the spread.

If You Are Dealing with Call and Put Options, Embrace the Underlying Stock's Trend

As an investor and trader in options, you need to consider the trend of the underlying stock as your friend. This means that you should not fight it. Basically, if the stock price is headed upwards, you should find a strategy that is in tandem with this movement. If you oppose it, you are unlikely to win.

Similarly, if the stock is on a downward trend, then do not oppose this movement but try and find a strategy that will accommodate this trend. You need to understand, however, that this saying is intended to guide you but is not necessarily a rule. This means that you apply it even while you consider all other factors. For instance, the major news may have an immediate effect on the price trend of a stock or shares.

As a trader, you should learn to jump successfully on a trend and follow the crowds rather than go to extremes and oppose it.

When Trading Options, Watch Out for Earnings Release Dates

Call and put options are generally expensive with the price increases significantly if there is an earnings release announcement looming. The reason is that the anticipation of very good or very bad earnings reports will likely affect the stock price. When this is an underlying stock in an options trade, then you should adjust your trades appropriately.

As an example, stocks such as Google may rise insanely during the earnings announcement week only to dip significantly shortly thereafter. Consider Apple shares that were trading at $450 at the markets. Call options with Apple as the underlying stock were trading at $460. However, the market had targeted a price of $480 within 3 days, which did not happen. This cost investors' money. Such underlying assets are considered volatile due to the high increase in price, rapid drop shortly thereafter and related risk of losing money.

Chapter 11. How to Double or Triple Your Returns

You are the one responsible for turning your venture into foreign exchange into a successful endeavor. That is one of the great things about the stock. You do not have a boss screaming down your neck, telling you to do something you do not agree with. You can come up with your trading plan based on your own research and your knowledge. That being said, success can come more quickly for some than for others, and a lot of the time, this has to do with approaching this endeavor with the right strategy. We will provide you with three strategies designed to help you make this stock as profitable as possible (with as little loss as possible).

Buy Low and Sell High

If you began stock trading today with $25,000 in your pocket and access to a trading platform, all ready and raring to go, how would you know what is low and what is high? It's your first day. Naturally, for you to understand what would represent a good low investment and conversely what is high, you need to know the exchange rate history of that currency. Maybe the exchange rate for the Japanese yen seems low, but actually, compared to last year or a few months ago, it's a little high. Now it would not be a good time to buy.

Maybe the pound seems low right now, but yesterday the British government announced that the first round of the Brexit negotiations with the EU failed, and therefore, the pound may have room to go lower than it is when you logged onto your trading platform. You can wait and see what the pound is today or tomorrow and buy then.

The point here is that buying low and selling high requires understanding the patterns associated with that stock and what might cause it to go up or down. And that's merely the buying side of things. Once you have bought low, you need to figure out when you are going to sell. This is where a good trading plan will come into play. A good plan will prevent you from selling too soon, or even not selling soon enough.

Focus on Not Losing Money Rather Than on Making Money

This may not be an easy strategy to understand initially, in part because not losing money and making money seem like two sides of the same coin. They are, but they are not identical. One of the personality types that is associated with difficulty in finding success in trading is the impulsive type. This type of person wants to make money and they want to make it quick. They have a vague strategy about how they plan on doing that, but the most important thing to them is that they have a high account balance to make as many trades as they need to turn a profit. This is the wrong approach. Currencies are not the same as stocks. A stock's value may change very little even over a week, so the strategy that involves a lot of trades to make money is usually not the best strategy. You need a clear idea of when you are going to but, yes, because you want to make money, but mostly because you don't want to lose.

Every market that involves exchanges, like the stock market, has some implicit risk, and stock trading is risky, too, because you may be tempted to give up the advantage you have to try and make money quickly.

Develop a Sense of Sentiment Analysis

All right, the third strategy was going to be about Fibonacci retracement, which is a type of technical analysis of the market, but as this is the basics of stock trading, we are going to go into a different strategy that is not any easier than a Fibonacci retracement, just different. Sentiment analysis is a term that is used in many different specialties, not just finance, and it is not easy to describe.

It is essentially a type of analysis that is not based on a chart showing exchange rates over time (technical analysis) or understanding a factor that might today be affecting the value of the stock(fundamental analysis). Sentiment analysis attempts to gauge the tone of the market, the direction the market is heading in, by parsing all of the available information.

A key to understanding sentiment analysis is likening it to public opinion. The economy may be booming, people have more money in their pocket, so this hypothetical country's stock should increase in value, but maybe it doesn't. Maybe there is something that is causing the market to be bearish, which might cause the stock to drop.

As you perhaps can tell, as this analysis is not based on any concrete information, it can be thought of as intuitive and no one has intuition on day 1. Let's be honest about that.

Intuition comes from experience. But the purpose of this strategy is to introduce to you the idea that not the foreign exchange market, like any market, is not going to behave like a machine because it's not a machine.

Markets are places where human beings come together and humans are unpredictable, often in a frustrating way. Perhaps one day, stock trading may be handled by machines (that wouldn't be fun), but that day is far off and so you will have to develop your own sense of where the market seems to be going and use this as a strategy to achieve success in this endeavor.

Regardless of the investment that you make, be sure always to do your research. Doing research is a must. It is what will increase your chances of making the right investment decision.

The more that you understand something, the more likely it that you will be able to predict how it will move in the market. This is why doing research is essential. It will allow you to know if something is worth investing in or not. Remember that you are dealing with a continuously moving market, so it is only right that you keep yourself updated with the latest developments and changes. The way to do this is by doing research.

Whether you will start forex trading or trade in general, it is always good to have a plan. Make sure to set a clear direction for yourself. This is also an excellent way to avoid being controlled by your emotions or becoming greedy. You should have a short-term plan and a long-term plan. You should also be ready for any form of contingency.

Make your plans practical and reasonable. Remember that you ought to stick to whatever project you come up with, so be sure to keep your ideas real. Before you come up with an idea, you must first have quality information. Again, this is why doing research is very important.

What if you fail to execute your plan? This is not uncommon. If this happens to you, relax and think about what made you fail to stick to your plan? Was it favorable to you or not? Take some time to analyze the situation and learn as much as you can from it. Indeed, having a plan is different from executing it. It is more challenging to implement a plan as it demands that you take positive actions.

Learn from Your Competitors

Pay attention to your competitors and learn from them. Studying your competitors is also an excellent way to identify your strengths and weaknesses. You can learn a great deal from your competitors, especially ideas on how you can better improve your business.

Your competitors can also help you promote your trading goals and draw more techniques. This way, you get a better idea of how to trade. You do not have to fight against your competitors; you can work together.

It is prevalent for people online to support one another. , it is a good practice that you connect with other traders, especially those who are in the same niche. Do not think of them as your direct competitors, and you might be surprised just how friendly they can be.

Now, a common mistake is to consider yourself always better than others. This is wrong as you are only deluding yourself, making you fail to see the bigger picture. Instead of still seeing yourself better than your competitors, learn from them, and see how you can use this knowledge to improve your trading endeavors.

Cash-Out

Some people who trade forex or invest in cryptocurrency commit the mistake of not making a withdrawal. The reason why they do not cash out is so that they can grow their funds. Since you can only earn a percentage of what you are trading/investing, having more funds in your account means making a higher profit return. Although this may seem reasonable, it is not a recommended approach. It is strongly advised that you should request a withdrawal. You should understand that the only way to enjoy your profits is by turning them into cash; otherwise, it is only as if you were using a demo account. Also, by making a withdrawal, you lower your risks since the funds you withdraw will no longer be exposed to risks.

You do not have to remove all your profits right away. If you want, you can withdraw 30% of your total profits, allowing the remaining 70% to add up to the funds in your account. The important thing is to make a withdrawal still now and then.

Take a Break and Have Fun

Making money online can be exciting and fun but it can also be a tiring journey. Therefore, give yourself a chance to take a break from time to time. When you take a break, do not spend that time thinking about your online business. Instead, you should spend it to relax your body and clear your mind. You will be more able to function more effectively if you do this. This is an excellent time to go on a vacation with your family or friends or at least enjoy a movie night at home. Do something fun that will put your mind off of business for a while. Do not worry; after this short break, and you are expected to work even more.

Making money online is a long journey, so enjoy it. Making money online can be lots of fun. Do not just connect with people to build a good following, but also try to make friends with your connections. You do not have to take things too seriously. Keep it fun and exciting.

Chapter 12. How to Become Millionaire with Option Trading

Most investors and traders at the securities markets often aim to buy low then sell high and make a profit. However, options traders are the key layers in any market. This is because they can earn large amounts of money regardless of market conditions.

The options traders can make money in any market environment, even where there are no trades up or down. The reason is that options contracts are flexible in different ways. This versatility is what makes them such powerful market tools for continued profitability. Here are some profitable approaches that you can adopt to become a millionaire with option trading

Writing Options

One of the best ways of winning at options is to write options. You can write some pretty sophisticated strategies which are capable of earning your top dollars.

As a writer, you get to earn what is known as a premium. This is money that you earn even if the investor does not eventually use it. It is possible to write profitable commodities-based options regularly. Speculators can come up with profitable options that they believe will fare well in the options markets.

The Straddle Strategy

This is another approach that can help you get rich with options trading. Options mostly involve the buying of security that then turns profitable when the underlying commodity moves in a particular direction. It could be up or down but all that is necessary is a movement. A straddle is a great choice of options investment vehicle because it does not desire a specific outcome as is the case in other situations.

With a straddle, you can purchase both calls and put options with the same expiry dates and at similar strike times. The straddle strategy can be successful if and only if the underlying security of the option sees movement in either direction just so long as the movement is sufficiently large to cover the cost of premiums in both directions. Speculators can write straddle options if they believe that it is going to do well in the market.

The Collar Strategy

We also have a strategy known as the collar strategy. It is considered a pretty challenging options strategy to understand. However, a seasoned speculator can write one for you but only if he owns the underlying asset. By owning the asset, he can take the risk.

In this instance, the best option is an out-of-the-money put option. This is beneficial because should the commodity price go down, then the losses will only be minimal as it is a put option. However, should the commodity move upwards, then the trader will make a tidy profit.

The Strangle Strategy

The strangle strategy is in some ways similar to the straddle. This is because they both include the buying of a call and put option as well as the same expiration date. The only difference is that they have different strike prices. For speculators, it is possible to use the information available to enter a low-cost position.

When a trader or speculator opts for this strategy, they choose a low-cost entry because either or both of the options contracts may be bought out-of-the-money. As such, it may not be worthwhile exercising the right afforded by the shares. Both the straddle and strangle can be written by a speculator or even the trader.

So, what is the Most Profitable Options Strategy?

We have now looked at several options trading strategies, all of which are profitable and easy to execute. There are more than 40 different variations of options trading techniques. This makes it a pretty difficult job to determine the most profitable options trading strategy.

A lot of the time, traders try to find trades that will not lose their money. Also, there is a lot of varied opinions out there about the best and most profitable strategies. Fortunately, most options trading strategies offer very attractive returns with huge margins being quite common. However, it can be a risky venture, so it is advisable to proceed with caution even as you seek to become a wealthy millionaire.

Options Trading is Quite Profitable

Some express concern about profitability as well as risks posed by options trading. Fortunately, it has been proven, over the years, to be quite profitable.

Trade-in options provide you with leverage which offers you the inherent right to control a huge number of shares. This kind of leverage offers returns far greater than what selling stocks only can offer.

If you can make use of the leverage afforded by stock options, then you stand a great chance of making huge profits. These are profits made from just minuscule movements of the underlying stocks. By identifying the right strategies, then you will be able to make money regardless of the prevailing market conditions.

This means making profits even when there is no movement in the market. However, with some strategies, you may lose money if you make a wrong move. Therefore, sufficient care needs to be taken to mitigate any such losses as they can be significant.

The Most Profitable Options Trading Strategy

It is advisable, to begin with, the most basic options trading strategies first. This is the way most options traders start. By using these simple options trading strategies, you stand to make huge returns on your investments and trading skills. It is very possible to enjoy a 100% return on investment within a couple of days and sometimes even in just a couple of hours.

You can also find plenty of websites and advisory services that provide advisory services and trading assistance to traders. Some trades may fail. But it is also likely that most of your trades will be successful. Therefore, a good strategy, or approach to this challenge would be to ensure you place multiple trades on each occasion. Ensure that your strategy will win you money even though one or two trades may lose some money.

What you need to do to achieve this level of success is to work hard on your technical analysis skills. With excellent analysis skills, you will be able to analyze trades and be able to accurately determine which ones are winners and which ones you should possibly avoid. Therefore, learn to use your technical analysis tools and skills and then put them to practice often. It is only with deep knowledge of technical analysis and lots of practice that you will then be able to hone your skills and become and wealthy and successful options trader.

Consistently Profitable Strategies – Selling Puts & Credit Spreads

There are some studies conducted by credible institutions that the two most profitable options trading strategies are selling credit spreads and selling put options. The study found that the profits from such trades are consistent and regular over a long period.

However, the study found something else. The study reveals that buying call options and put options is more profitable in the long run even though it is not as consistent. You stand to make 7%-12% per month on the total portfolio which is about 84% to over 144% per annum. Considering that the techniques used are very simple, easy to apply, and require the most basic of technical analysis, then your chances of making stress-free money are very high. You can expect to win over 80% of your trades if you come up with the right trading plan.

Overall Best Options Trading Strategy

According to finds, it is widely accepted that you will make the most profits selling puts. If you invested a lot of your trading resources into selling put options, then you stand to make a lot of money consistently and with very little risk of loss.

The only challenge with the selling option is that it has certain limitations. This is because selling put options works best in a market that trends upwards or is on the rise. You can complement selling puts with selling ITM puts for long-term contracts. These are contracts that last 6 months or longer. They will make you tons of money simply because of the effect of time decay.

Also, when you sell, as a trader on the options market, credit spreads, you will be able to take advantage of the market in both directions. This means you will profit from an upward as well as downward market trend. This is great as even smaller traders can make some money regardless of experience. Therefore, always remember not to search for the size of the profits. When searching for the most profitable and successful options strategy, focus on factors like;

- Ability to come up with a reliable and safe plan

- Have a plan that generates regular income

- Associated risks are low

- Technical requirements are manageable

Sell Naked Puts is one of the most lucrative ways of making money trading options. The return on margin is almost as lucrative as selling credit spreads. However, it does not carry a similar level of risk. In short, anytime that you sell a put option, then you make it possible to purchase a stock at a price of your choosing.

A Closer Look at Naked Puts

It's the end of June and XYZ stock is at $50. However, the market is fluctuating and you prefer to buy this stock for $45. What you need to do at this stage is to sell a $45 put option for $2. You can put the expiration date on this option as the third week of July. Once you post the option, you will immediately receive $200 into your trading account. Now should the XYZ stock price fall below $45, you will be required to purchase 100 units. This will cost you $4,500.

However, you already have $200 in your account so the cost of buying the shares is reduced by this amount. If you sell a put option each month for the following six months, you will receive a total of $1,200. This will drastically lower the cost of buying XYZ shares. However, if the stock starts rising, you will not need to buy it but will keep selling the put option. While there is a slight risk due to liquidity issues, this strategy is quite a winner and can lead you to immense profits in just a short while.

ROI or Return on Investment

The Term ROI stands for Return on Investment. ROI is a measure of performance and is used by both investors and traders to measure the effectiveness and efficiency of an investment. This includes your trading capital. ROI deliberately endeavors to measure directly the total return derived from a particular investment.

For instance, if you invest a total of X amount on a particular trade and then received a return of Y from this investment, then ROI will endeavor to indicate the performance of your investment amount and what you received for your efforts. If you want to calculate the rate of return of an investment, you will need to know the total return which is then divided by the investment amount.

One of the most important aspects of your investment portfolio is its profitability. You need to regularly monitor your investments which are best achieved using the ROI or return on investment. It is advisable to work out what each dollar invested has generated.

R.O.I = (Profits — Costs) / Costs

Even then, investors need to understand that the ROI depends on numerous other factors such as the kind of investment security preferred and so on. Also, note that a high ROI implies a higher risk while a lower means reduced risk. For this reason, appropriate risk management must be undertaken.

Chapter 13. How COVID-19 Will Affect Option Trading

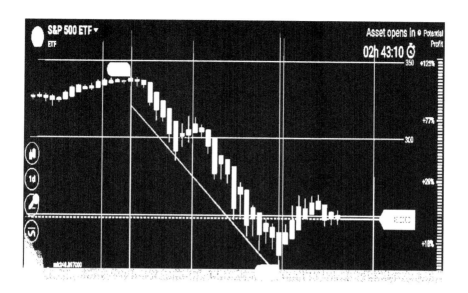

Coronavirus has had a variety of effects on global financial markets. It's difficult to say to what extent the epidemic affected people now that it's not over; between February 19 and March 23, the S & P 500 lost more than a third of its value. Over the same time frame, the Dow Jones Industrial Average has lost even more (up to 36 percent). Despite the return to growth, both indicators point to a massive disruption in the global economy that hasn't been seen in the last five years. Furthermore, the economic effects of the world's most recent pandemic may not be limited to that. It's likely that there are already undiscovered or delayed effects that will be found later.

Despite the recent recovery, the economic downturn in China, the United States, and Europe still have the potential to cause a full-fledged financial crisis. The current year's global GDP is very likely to experience a setback.

What should we expect?

The 'Fast Recovery' scenario, according to Roland Berger, an independent European consulting firm, is already out of the question. Their experts also predict that the outage will last between 4 and 12 weeks. China has moved further down the coronavirus curve, and its economy has regained its foothold (at least, according to the Chinese government itself). COVID-19's results, on the other hand, are still unknown in Europe and the United States. It might take a lot of time for them to recover.

Certain sectors will be affected harder than the overall economy. Airlines, leisure, and retail (with the exception of FMCG) will be hit hard. The automobile, logistics, and oil/gas industries are all in the same boat. Financial services, on the other hand, would be significantly less impacted. Nonetheless, the pandemic's impacts would be felt to some degree by all sectors. It will definitely take some time for the global economy to recover.

The COVID-19 stay-at-home requirement has spawned a major sub-industry of options trading, which is increasing in tandem with a rise in equities trading that shows no signs of slowing down.

In November, stock options trading reached new highs, continuing a pattern that started earlier in the year.

On all options markets, equity options trading is up 50% year to date compared to last year.

Optional Equity (Volume)

- NASDAQ has a 49 percent market cap.

- CBOE has a 51% market share.

- ICE has a 58 percent share of the market.

"As you can see from the volumes, the public is accepting alternatives in a completely unparalleled manner," Interactive Brokers' Steve Sosnick told me. "I think the lockdown led to some of the popularity... Many people were stranded at home, with $1,200 checks or rent/loan moratoria, with no sports to watch or wager on. So they went to the stock market, where they discovered that options have payout mechanisms that are identical to sports bets."

The comparison to sports betting is intentional: "The psychology [of sports betting versus stock betting] is quite close." "With sports betting, I have a chance to win a portion of the money. It's the same with stocks and options, only there are thousands of bets you can make every day with stocks and options, and when you're in an upmarket like we have been, you can start to believe that the odds are really in your favor."

Most of the trading activity has happened in out-of-the-money options that are nearing expiration, with most of it day trading: purchasing in the morning and selling in the afternoon, according to Kyle Robinson, who monitors trading activity at Piper Sandler.

What makes you want to do that? "They're selling options because a lot of people don't have enough money to buy a lot of stocks," he said. "You can purchase options for a fraction of the price, and if your options move at the same percentage as the underlying stock, you can profit as if you owned it."

Many day traders are right to aim options trading, according to Sosnick, and are not behaving irrationally.

He pointed out that buying out of the money calls has low initial investment, so you can only lose what you put in. "You will only lose a dollar if you buy a call for a dollar." "They might be poorly capitalized," Sosnick hypothesized when asked why so many people are doing basic day trading, in the morning and out by the close. They might crave the opportunity to sleep at night. It's possible that it's their only option."

Zero commissions on many trades, as well as the presence of social media and chat rooms full of debates on high-profile names, are all contributing to the day trading phenomenon.

Another important aspect is the availability of instructional materials that instruct traders about how to trade options.

"We have seen no decline in interest in educational content on our website," says JJ Kinahan, TD Ameritrade's Chief Market Strategist. "Stock fundamentals and getting started with options are the two most popular videos on our site." He pointed out that viewing of that content is already three times higher than a year ago.

Equity Trading is Also on the Rise

The rise in options trading is being accompanied by a similar rise in stock trading. For example, trading volume at Fidelity increased by 97 percent year over year in the third quarter.

According to Rich Repetto of Piper Sandler, regular average revenue trades (DARTs) at Interactive Brokers increased by 174 percent in November compared to the same time last year. They have added 29,000 new accounts to their scheme.

In a recent note to clients, Repetto wrote, "We are raising our 4Q20 EPS forecast due to better than expected trading, continued account expansion, and good margin balance and customer equity growth."

Robinson noted that trading in futures contracts, which are more often used by practitioners as hedging vehicles, and index options have not seen the same drastic rise.

How long will this high level of trading last?

What could probably go wrong in the midst of all this bullish call buying? The greatest risk, according to Sosnick, is simple mean reversion: "You may get into a losing streak." "If you buy risky calls, it doesn't take much to lose money after a few days or weeks."

Sosnick also hypothesized that, regardless of market dynamics, all of this day trading might have a finite shelf life.

"I wonder how far does this has to do with the fact that many people haven't had to pay student loans in a long time and will have to do so next month," he said. "If you use the typical student loan payment of $400 to bring in the economy, and I have to start paying that back, that is money that will come out of the markets."

Robinson concurred. Robinson told me, "We don't expect these levels to last." "Those who have stayed at home will return to work once the pandemic is over. When the vaccine is released, volatility will likely decrease, making day trading more difficult."

Sosnick decided that if the large amount of call buying stopped, volatility would decrease. He pointed out that the massive amount of call buyers has inflated implied volatility, which is one of the reasons the CBOE Volatility Index (VIX) has remained trapped at the elevated 21 levels amid a major rally.

How many people will be around for the next round of corrections?

According to Sosnick, the next correction would be the ultimate test to see if these new traders hang around. "People are knowledgeable, and they are attempting to educate themselves. A full market cycle, on the other hand, is the best education for traders, and we haven't seen one yet. Many of these traders just entered the market after March, so they haven't seen the whole cycle."

Sosnick doesn't blame the younger generation for enjoying a good time with stocks and options when they can: "And betting on NASDAQ was much more likely to pay off than betting on the Jets," he joked.

Conclusion

Thank you for making it through to the end of this book. You've now had a careful stroll through the key standards and ventures in options trading we feel are fundamental to progress as an options trader. You've figured out how the options markets function, the best trading strategies and why it's basic to pick the best possible fundamental assets for the procedures you need to utilize. You've additionally observed that great exit strategies are nearly as imperative as discovering great trades to enter, that focusing on the points of interest is basic, and that achievement is virtually inconceivable without a decent money-management plan — and the discipline to follow it.

At last, you've got lots of pages loaded with vital inquiries to consider in your search for the best online options broker. At the end of the day, it's a great opportunity to control up, plugin — and profit. You have all the data you have to appreciate 24-hour access to the options markets, fast and programmed execution of your orders and the most reduced commissions in the history of options trading. In any case, to share these advantages, you should confront the bigger individual duties that accompany coordinated access to online trading.

You should have the discipline to do your very own research, screen your own positions and monitor every one of the points of interest you may leave to your full-benefit financial firm. You can never again depend on a broker to watch your positions and call with guidance or suggestions. You are currently an autonomous administrator — and, all things considered, must be absolutely in charge of your own behavior.

You should likewise be mindful and be prepared to react to both fast moves in everyday trading designs and consistently evolving longer-term economic situations.

In case you think tolerating such difficulties and practicing such discipline is simple, think of one as a little preventative portion of the real world. An investigation — "Online Investors: Do the Slow Die First?" by Brad M. Barber and Terrance Odean, published in Economic Intuition.

Printed in Great Britain
by Amazon